Pleasure the basic need of Human

notionpress.com

Pleasure
the basic need of
Human

R. N. Sahani

notionpress.com

Notion Press

Old No. 38, New No. 6
McNichols Road, Chetpet
Chennai - 600 031

First Published by Notion Press 2016

ISBN 978-93-5206-882-1

DEDICATED

This book is dedicated to every reader who has a burning desire to do something extraordinary and special in his life. Especially to those whose desire and concern are not limited to them only but revolves around the welfare of the society as a whole.

- Our acceptance become our destiny.
- Our gradual achievements make our acceptance strong.

Many people become successful in life and a huge number of people fail in their life. It doesn't mean that all the successful are talented and all the failed people are not talented. It simple means that average people are those who have accepted themselves as average while successful people have accepted themselves as successful. Success and failure are just our mental acceptance. Our acceptance makes us successful or failed, rich or poor. We can change our acceptance by systematic and gradual achievements. When our dream, action and belief are in one direction then miracle happens and divine power helps to attain our destination. Devine power lies in every individual, we have to just make our self aligned with this power inherited to every individual.

– R. N. Sahani

Contents

Preface

There are a number of books available in the market which claim to make one successful in considerable days, or may be thirty days or so. It is not only impossible, but also not normal which is applicable to everybody. Since, change in our thinking is not so easy that it can be brought about in such a short period of time. This book is intended to start a process of right thinking. It will help you understand how we can fabricate our destination by our habitual thinking. I have described many practical examples, suggesting that success is not difficult to be achieved but our wrong perception makes it so. It is not just a readymade capsule which will change your life within a few days. This book will help activating your thinking and thirst to discover your real potential. This book will enable you to find out how you are living with a wrong perception which keeps you an average. This is just my acceptance that I am an average person. This is just our acceptance that there are no options except our present job.

I have explained how an average and dropped out student who has entrepreneur ability hires the most talented people in his firm. It is very despairing that intellectuals mostly work under an entrepreneur. Risk-bearing capacity and foresightedness are the two very important qualities that mark a big difference between an employee and an employer. Ability to see opportunity and capability to implement his idea on the ground level despite of all the challenges are the basic quality which differentiate them from the mass people.

Unfortunately, goal orientation is the prime focus and strategy of work for any concern. This is something that makes our job boring and painful and the quality and quantity of our work decrease. The prime focus of this book is to develop a pleasure-oriented work which enhances the quality of work and makes it joyful. Work then becomes a game and we enjoy it. We have forgotten how we were so fun loving from our childhood. The saddest thing is that now we don't even take a game as a game. We have made everything serious. We have forgotten our fun-loving nature gifted by God.

Development and changes start only when we understand how we are fabricating our destiny. Until then we don't understand that we are the factors which creates our destiny, we can't do anything. Right conception and right perception are the two very essential pillars on which a strong and sustainable personality development happens.

A testy recipe doesn't require a hard work or very smart personality but it is just a skill which is developed by a regular practice. Any skill is an art which requires practice and once the skilled is develops it become a natural act.

Our physical body and behaviour are just a hardware which is controlled by the software that is our perception and our acceptance. This perception and acceptance can be change in our mind just like installing software in computer, but this process is gradual. It is interesting to know that millions of people travel every year to pilgrims and many great worship places for getting blessing from god to have a prosperous and happy life which may fulfil their dream and desire. The take a lot of pains and invest a huge money and time in this process, but unfortunately nobody thinks to change his habitual thinking and behaviour which are the key factors of changing their destiny.

1. Pleasure: The Basic Need

1.01 BASIC NEED OF HUMAN

Every individual in this world wants to be something different from what he presently is. Change is an inherited desire of human being. Everybody wants to be successful but not everyone is successful. Most of the people have a general mindset that being successful is very tough. No! Actually every human being has some basic instincts which work as a driving force for everything.

As the holy book Geeta teaches us *"NiskamKaramyoga."* It means just keep on doing your duty without thinking about the results. Many schools and colleges display these basic messages of the Geeta very prominently, but the fact is that their conduct is quite different to these basic messages. Our modern education system is not aligned with the basic principles of Geeta. Moreover, they generally contradict these principles.

Today, thousands of motivational books teach us how to make an effective goal and the process to accomplish these goals. Determination of a firm goal and its accomplishment are very important factors that make one's life worth living. Most of us believe that if one does not work on the proper setting of his goal, he cannot be successful. Till a few decades back, Ramayana and Geeta had a major impact in human Sanskara and conduct of a major chunk of Indian society.

Now, the time has changed and so has our way of thinking. Our life style has changed considerably as the technological development has taken place. The materialistic approach is a prominent deciding factor that decides our pattern of thinking and behaviour. I inspected that there is a shift in the tendency of modern society from "Niskam Karamyoga" to modern goal-setting attitude. Before you get me wrong, let me be very clear that I am not against the working style of goal setting. I just want to study the basic human tendency, which is responsible for such mind shift and change of behaviour pattern.

The basic desires of human:

1. Survival instinct
2. Pleasure instinct
3. Desire to prove "He is the best"

1.02 SURVIVAL INSTINCT

A plant grows if it is protected and watered regularly, and later it gives pleasure. Growth and pleasure both are closely related and interdependent. Millions of seeds develop in a tree and the tree makes different arrangements to disperse the seeds all around. Even a tree knows that if all the seeds fall under it, all will die and the desire of the tree to create new plants will not be fulfilled. Thousands of different variety of fruits and grains are available to us only due to the strong desire of plants to keep alive generation to generation. Every new plant or a new baby carries the same tendency to keep it alive and transfer it to the new generation.

Expansion is the law of nature. Let us study how this tendency works on the formation and expansion of any religious group? Many religions emerged in the world history and a few have survived and expanded while many others were eliminated. It is interesting that why and how, many religions could not survive and disappeared from this world. To understand this, we must understand the two most important religious practices.

i. Religious acts and their strong rituals
ii. Aggressive expansion policies

People may be broadly categorized into two categories:

1. People who involve in religious act;
2. People who are focused in the act of expansion of the religion.

The second category is the key factor due to which any religion expands in the world rapidly. These categories are so fanatic and so passionate towards the expansion of the religion, usually go to any extent. They even kill a huge mass if people are not obeying their views. Many religion shave spread widely around the world because of these fellows. Their ego is satisfied in both ways: their belief is accepted by others, and they are doing a great job for their religion. These satisfactions make them very cruel. The saddest thing is that many people who are treated as the scholar of the religion acknowledge and encourage these activities.

Religion must be used for enhancement in the quality of life. It should be used for enhancement of our wisdom and brotherhood between people. Actual purpose of the religion is to spread love and friendship among the human being. It is not to be restricted only to human but it gives sympathy to every life on this earth. Instead, it is used to protect our ego, and that is why fights are going throughout the world since ancient times.

The people who have very much enthusiasm in spreading the religion have no concern and interest for following the real message of the religion. Basically, it happens due to the direction of flow of their energy towards expansion alone.

Whatever we do is motivated by our "desire of pleasure." Whatever the activity may be, it is basically compelled by our basic need of desire of pleasure. In general, we involve ourselves more in activities which give us more pleasure. From this, we can see that we are attracted towards pleasure and distracted from pain. We can also say that it is the principle of "pain or pleasure" which guides ourselves.

1.03 DIFFERENT GAMES CHATTER THE NEED OF PLEASURE

Just think. Many types of games had been played from ancient times. Very earlier, it was very simple. But, as our civilization grew and became advanced, the type and complexity of games have also developed greatly. No one can deny the importance of game in human civilization. The basic question is why game has been a very important thing in human life from ancient times? The answer is very interesting. Game satisfies our need to prove oneself, that is, "I am the best." The basic purpose is to win the game, and he who wins proves that he is the best among all. Also, his basic desire fulfils that he is the best.

An athlete practices his painful exercises day and night. People may feel surprised about the motivation which makes him motivated so long to keep doing his practices years after years. It is obvious that he is motivated by the feeling that one day he will fulfil his strong desire to prove "He is the best."

"Pain and pleasure are basic factors of our motivation. Whatever we do, we do to get pleasure or to avoid pain"

Another interesting factor is to demonstrate our achievement and to hide our failure. Everyone knows that achievers are awarded and facilitated in the presence of thousand people. To facilitate this psychological need, prize is generally given at the time of any celebration or at any function. The pleasure of any achiever multiplies many times when it is acknowledged by huge number of people. Why does this happen? Acknowledgement by huge number of people shows that he is the best among all those people who not only witness his achievement but also accepts his best performance.

When we are eager to show our achievements then obviously we will hide our failure since it will go against our need to prove us the best. Hiding our failure comes in our mind from our childhood. For example, any child who has fallen from his cycle gets up immediately and first assures that nobody had seen him while he has fallen down.

Every person has some pleasure and many pains in their life. But the question is we don't do anything for pain but still, why most of the people's life is filled with so much pain? Really it is very interesting to know why it happens that we work for pleasure but we get pain. Every person does a lot of activity for pleasure but its real effect comes after sometime. To understand this, we have to understand the principle of "long run effect." Let us take an example of an athlete who practices the painful exercise daily on a regular basis. At initial stage, he passes through lots of pain, but his health and performance grows day by day and one day he becomes a great athlete and wins a lot of medals, name and fame countrywide and in many cases worldwide. This is an example of long run effect. Let us consider another example in which a person smokes daily for pleasure. Day by day his health deteriorates and his money gets wasted. One day he becomes so helpless and his life becomes so painful and filled with pain due to health problem. He didn't invite pain in his life directly, but his act actually invited pain in long run. So, it is very important that we need to understand that how the activity we are doing now will affect our life. If the answer is positive then it must be done and if the answer is negative then it must be stopped immediately.

We must be aware for our everyday activities

Some activities start with pain and give a lot of pleasure in the long run.

Some activities start with pleasure and give lots of pain in the long run.

Now come to our education pattern which is completely based on the spirit of competition. One point which I want to express is that every religion teaches us to love each other, whereas our education system teaches us competition in which we have to win the race against others. This feeling, not intentionally, develops a feeling of hate. What a contradiction between our religious teachings and our education system! This feeling of completion makes a student focused to his results. His complete focus on result makes him defocused from his studies. He loses his interest and enthusiasm in his study and his study process becomes a boring job. Now think about a student who involves himself in studies the whole year. After one year he gets top rank in his class. Now it very clear that his whole study process would be a boring job. It is only the day of result and few days that he feels happiness. He again starts his studies for his next year and the painful process starts again. On an average more than 95% of the work he does is not much interesting for him. But my question is, is there no other option or way of preparation? Of course, there is another way of thinking and way of working.

"When the quality and quantity improves, the results will be the best.

Doesn't work for just for the result, but work for pleasure?"

First, we have to know that pleasure and pain basically depends on the way of our thinking. What is our approach towards our job which is assigned to me? Whatever we do and whatever we think about the job is the basic cause which makes our job painful or pleasure. In the example of the student, if he shifts his focus from good grades to learning new things, then what will happen? If our approach is focused on learning new things, then immediately it will become very interesting since every day we will learn something new and interesting. This interest will make one more involved and focused day by day. The quality and quantity of his learning skills will improve greatly. Automatically his deep study will be reflected in his result. This will change everything like our involvement, our enjoyment and our result. Now, he is getting pleasure every day and every time he learns a new thing. Now, his pleasure is not limited only to the few days of results. The entire year, he will enjoy his study process due to the change in his approach towards his studies.

At work places, we find a few people who have no interest in the job which is assigned to them. He just works in a pressure. Lack of interest in a job makes the job very boring and very difficult. He works without any interest and at evening he feels tired. If you perform a boring job, then you will feel yourself quite exhausted, it is very natural. Such employee always complains that too much job is assigned for him. This is not the fact. This is his wrong perception, which has developed due to his wrong approach towards his work. His lack of interest in job makes him frustrated and he feels that the work is huge. It is very easy to understand this mentality. The feeling is like we have to wait for a train for three hours and everyone knows how painful it is. But we don't realize how the same three hours passes in a cinema hall. This is the way how our mind thinks.

In this world nobody is lazy. But the person who looks like lazy is an unfortunate person who couldn't find a job suited to his passion or talent. It is very important to know what his passion is. If he couldn't find his passion or he couldn't find a job suited to his passion then his potential will remain dormant. Suppose a young person joins a job, not of his interest, at the age of twenty-five and if he works for the organization to the age of sixty years then he will pass his whole service life of thirty-five years just like a punishment. It is obvious that if a person feels that he has to do a lot of work due to pressure everyday then it is not different from a punishment. Many people use liquors just to escape from the pain of their job. I don't mean every liquor user uses it for this frustration but of course job frustration is also one of the major reasons.

Let us think what is the practical solution of this problem? If we talk about the solution then everyone should be engaged in a job suited to his passion for optimum productivity and optimum job satisfaction. But practically this is not possible. Then what is the option? From the point of view of an employee he must change his job and should go for another company which is better suitable for his passion. But unfortunately this option is also not possible for everyone. Then what are the other alternatives. It is very simple and very easily applicable to everyone by applying just some simple techniques.

Earlier, we have talked that the way we think makes our job painful or pleasurable. If we simply change the way of thinking about our jobs, immediately our feeling and realization will change. For example, a person deals 100 customers every day and he makes himself exhausted in dealing 100 people. Instead, if he thinks that he has an opportunity to obelise 100 people in a single day, then the feeling itself gives him pleasure.

An effective option is to develop interest in our present job. I think this one is a very practical solution which is suitable to every person. This is just like wearing a leather shoe to protect out feet instead of covering the whole earth by leather. It is just like adjusting our sail according to the wind. When our approach changes the same job becomes joyful.

Our simple concern should be to make any process enjoyable which match with the basic need of human psychology. What happens when we make our work enjoyable?

1. Work appears like a game
2. In game, we won't get tired, we just enjoy
3. We get reward daily
4. Involvement of our inner mind, multiplies our output

We can change our approach towards work by changing our approach. When we work for a goal, work becomes a boring. However, when we work for the growth or for learning skill and competence, work becomes joyful every day.

Performance speaks loudly.

Performance gets exposed

Publicly acceptance increases

Happiness increases

Focus on future goal decreases involvement in the process of work.

Performance decreases

Achievements decreases

Frustration increases

1.04 PAIN AND PLEASURE

Pain and pleasure are the very important factors which control our pattern of thinking and behaviour. Our pleasure is basically correlated to our desire. A human being grown up in a society learns many things from the environment and from the association where he grew up. A number of small and big desires develop in our mind. When we achieve our desired things, then a wave of satisfaction develops in our mind. When something happens against our desire then a wave of dissatisfaction develops in our mind, the pain. When our big and powerful desire is fulfilled then very powerful waves arise in our mind.

As we understand, pleasure is nothing but just a wave that rises in our mind. Then as the intensity of the wave becomes weak and vanishes gradually, our mental waves also gradually loses its intensity and finally finishes completely. This is not only applicable to our pleasure but also applicable to pain in same way. That is why, the intensity of pleasure decreases gradually. It means that anything or event won't remain as a pleasant thing forever. Suppose a person purchases his dream car for which he used to dream from his childhood. When he brought his dream car, he feels himself over the sky due to his great pleasure as he has brought his dream car to home. He becomes so eager and exited to share and show his new car to his friends and relatives. But this excitement gradually fades away. After few months, his level of excitement decreases to a normal stage. And then his car doesn't give him much pleasure and excitement as when it was new when he brought it to his home.

The same thing applies to unwanted things which happen in our life. If wife or husband dies accidentally, the remaining partner either wife or husband passes through unbearable pain in his life. He feels that he will not be surviving after the death of his life partner. But this acute pain gradually normalizes and he accustoms to live with the painful memory of his life partner. In both cases, our joy and sorrow creates a wave in our mind and the intensity of the waves normalizes gradually. So we can conclude that

"Nothing, joy or sorrow, is permanent."

As we discussed, successful people make constructive work as their habit, whereas unsuccessful people make the unproductive work as their habit. Anything we make as our habit becomes very effective.

Two factors which help to keep us involved in any activity.

- Achievement in process
- Process becomes a habit
- Some value addition in process

It is obvious that any activity becomes very joyful if we get some achievement in that particular activity. Achievement makes us greatly motivated to do that particular activity. But achievement doesn't happen at initial stages. It is very difficult to persist in the activity. We should not give up doing the activity.

It is just like a plant which gives flowers and fruits only after the full maturity of the plant. Before that we have to put lots of efforts to keep the plant survive and grow properly.

Patience and enjoyment in the process are the key factors which keep us motivated to keep on the process persistently. If any person has no patience and no approach to enjoy the process, then he will quit in very early stages.

We can continue the activity despite of any achievement if we have cultivated a habit in our activity. If the particular activity becomes our habit then only we can do it at regular basis. So, a very important factor which makes a man successful that is his ability to make his habit, which is very important and useful. For example, most of the people used to take bath daily. Though it doesn't give any achievement, people use to take bath daily only due to their habit.

In third case, if it is not the stages to give any achievement and it is not a habit, then what has to be done to keep on doing the work? In the absence of achievement and habit, the work process will be very dull and it will be difficult to persist. Then the one thing which will be helpful to increase our involvement is "process of value addition." This is the method by which our interest will get continued to that particular activity.

1.05 ACTION, LEARNING, ACHIEVEMENT AND PLEASURE

A small group of staff in my office decided to play carom board at their free time during lunch hour. All of them were average and below average players. Gradually, I realized that our accuracy in hitting has been increasing day by day. The game became more joyful as their accuracy increased. I found that their involvement and interest in the game increased too much. Then they started thinking of organizing a tournament in the office. Their too much involvement started hampering their own allotted jobs. The department realized that this excessive involvement is hampering the normal day to day works. It decided to stop the game completely in the premises. This sudden prohibition on the game made the staff frustrated and created a feeling of dissatisfaction. After all, they had to obey the instructions of the management and couldn't start the game in the office again.

A few months later on an extra work on Sunday, the manager allowed us to play carom that was the time I realized how our skill and efficiency level decreased and reached to almost the initial level.

This cycle gives a great lesson about our learning process. I derived a formula for success in any field of life. The formula is A L A P

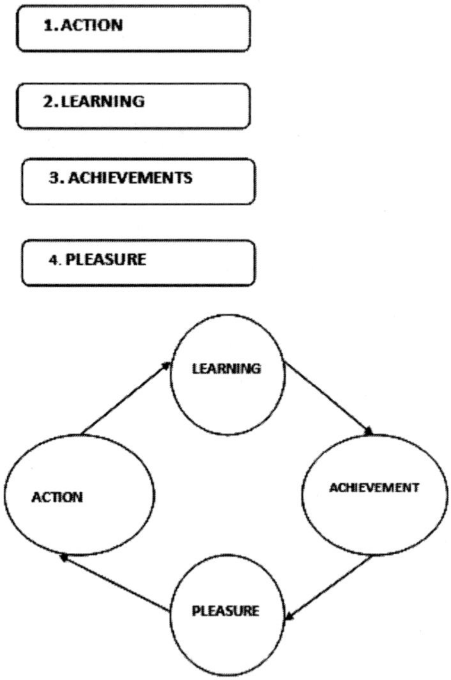

Initially, all the players were on average, but as they started playing they started learning and their skills increased gradually. As their accuracy in hitting increased they started to earn more scores. Earning scores developed a feeling of achievement. This feeling of achievement pleased them. This pleasure involved them more and more to the game. Their more involvement in the game increased their learning and increased their accuracy in hitting. This way the cycle gained speed and their involvement, learning, achievement and pleasure increased day by day.

JUST PICK UP A GAME AND PLAY MORE AND MORE

YOU WILL LEARN MORE AND MORE

YOUWILL WIN MORE AND MORE

YOU WILL ENJOY MORE AND MORE

AGAIN YOU WILL PLAY MORE

AND THIS CYCLE KEEPS ON GOING

Later on, this cycle will rotate automatically without much effort and the interesting thing is difficult to stop it, which is easily understood by the "Law of Inertia."

Another interesting thing which I realized was, as the game started, the skills and accuracy increased earlier but after discontinuation skill and accuracy decreased to almost the initial level. Their efficiency level decreased again and reached to their initial level which was visible when the game was started again.

OX axis represents time

OY axis represents efficiency

Y PEAK LEVEL OF EFFICIENCY

GRADUALLY REACHED TO ORIGINAL LEVEL OF

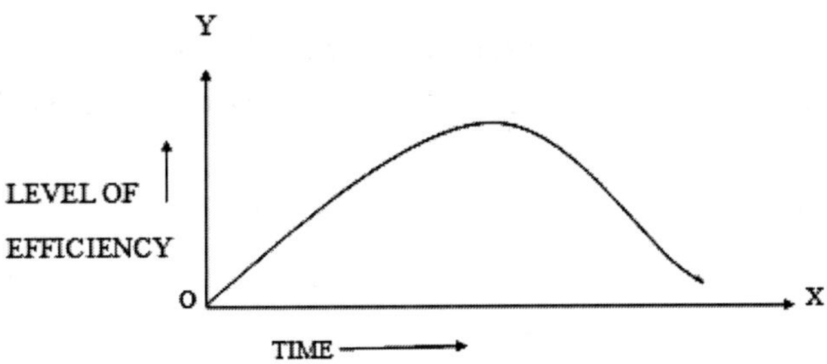

I found 'ALAP' applicable in every field of our life.

Achievement has a very strong binding force which binds any performer in a field. Apparently, it seems that achievement binds us to perform more and more. In fact, it's not the achievement but the joy that we derive from our achievements. Why does pleasure bind us so strongly? The answer is simple which we have discussed earlier:

"Pleasure is our basic need. Whenever this basic need is fulfilled we get motivated."

1.06 PLEASURE OF LOVE AND EGO

There is a basic difference between the feeling of love and feeling of ego. Parent bears lot of pain just to provide comfort and happiness to their children. They feel pleasure even in painful situation. This pleasure basically comes from the feeling of love and affection to their children. Whatever we do gives pleasure if it is derived by the feeling of love.

There is a very simple idea, that is feeling of love compels us to give something, while feeling of ego and hate, compels us to snatch something from other. When love increases the circle of our concern to other increases, but as ego increases then the circle of our concern decreases to you. Giving something to other is a divine feeling, which is closely related to the constructive forces of universe.

"Our area of concern expands with the feeling of love. But ego decreases our area of concern"

Our desire to grab something from other is just like a beggar mindset. A beggar mindset always feels like something is lacking in his life. Our belief and actual feelings attract similar things in our life. In addition, his feeling of lacking creates lacking in his life in many ways. However, feeling to do something for other and to give something to other is the mindset of a king, which is filled with prosperity, happiness and joy. Helping others with expectation is not a help, but just an investment.

"Helping others with some expectation is not a help, but it is just an investment"

Suppose you find a hare which is injured. You bring it home and dress its wound. Gradually it gets healed, and the hare becomes your friend. Now everyday he lives with you and plays with you. Can you imagine the satisfaction and pleasure since you have saved someone's life? This is incomparable to any things. No money and other commodities will be able to provide you such satisfaction.

In today's lifestyle, the pleasure of giving has minimized due to our materialistic approach. The tendency to take something to other has increased very much. If you focus, much about getting something from other then the giving tendency will decrease. If we focus on giving something to others then the tendency to take will decrease automatically.

Now let us think about the law of universe. When our approach to gain more from others increases, then others become cautious, and they go away from us. Our gaining approach makes people keep away from us. The approach of other people towards us changes because of our gaining approach towards them.

Till date, we have a tendency to get something from others and people gradually get away from us due to our greedy nature. Now, just reverse the process, don't think to get something. Instead think what I can give them and how I can give them. Suddenly, you will feel miraculous change in their behaviour. All those who were escaping from us are gradually coming closer; not to get something, but to return back something.

- **Therefore the basic concept is what we want for us, just start to give others.**

RIGHT ATTITUDE

As we are aware, our way of thinking which is called attitude is the basic cause of making a job painful or filled with pleasure. Development of attitude is a long process which starts right from our childhood when we start to stand-up and make efforts to walk on our feet. It is just like computer software which is being loaded right from our childhood and it is upgraded and degraded time to time with every experiences of life. Now, first we understand about the basic facts which contribute in formation of our attitude.

1. Our home's environment
2. Our school's/working place's environment
3. Our friends circle
4. Own studies and thoughts

Two very important factors which play a crucial role in life:

1. Right attitude

The attitude needed to enjoy every situation and every work. If one just takes a challenge for themselves, he will enjoy every situation. Our habit and tendency play a very crucial role in success in any field. Successful person chooses some right things and makes it his tendency to do it every time, everywhere. Failure develops a negative tendency. The right tendency develops a man day by day while the failure person declines in his life day by day due to his wrong tendency.

Whatever we see we do not realize in an exact manner what we have actually seen, but our attitude combines with it and makes it a completely different thing. This combination of our own perception makes the things different either it may upgrade the things or degrade the things. Now the question is why it happens and how it happens? In addition, another question is how it affects our life?

What is attitude and how it is formed? This is a particular type of behaviour which we have practiced knowingly or unknowingly. This particular type of behaviour has been developed by repeated action due to some social or other environment. Let us take an example to understand the process of formation of attitude. One person always behaved with the other person very rudely and his son always keeps on seeing this particular behaviour. Unknowingly, he has taken it as a normal behaviour. He started to copy it since he is not at a stage to discriminate whether it is right or wrong? Unknowingly, he started to do the particular activity and gradually becomes master in particular behaviour. Later on this behaviour becomes his nature, becomes his natural activity. As his negative behaviour became a part of his life, it started to give the negative effect in his life in the form of ill behaviour. He couldn't understand the root cause of the present outcomes. Now, this ill behaviour is so natural in his life. He couldn't find his behaviour is wrong. He always thinks that the other person is wrong and becomes more violent. Lastly, when he realizes that there is something wrong in his pattern of behaviour, it is too late and very difficult to come out from his behaviour.

1.07 JUST ENJOY THE PROCESS

Now this is obvious that "Pleasure is the basic need of human life." Our thinking, activity and behaviour are driven by the need of pleasure. However, our life is full of many anxieties and unpleasant feelings. Unknowingly, we have created many problems and unpleasant things in our life which is against the basic principles of our life.

Now, what is the solution for the problems? We have created a lot of negative things in our thinking and behaviour pattern. All of these have been acquired by long gradual process. We need not have to fight with the negative things but just start the positives traits and pattern of thinking. It will take time and will establish in our habitual thinking gradually. As the positive things establish, the negative things will decrease gradually.

Creation of a positive thinking process is just like learning to drive a vehicle. We first know the right process of driving. Then we practice the different methods in the process of driving. Knowing the right process is not enough. It requires practice and to get mastery to apply it when it is required. This mastery is not developed in a few days. We gradually develop mastery in the different skills, and our driving becomes very smooth and makes us capable to handle all the difficult traffic situations.

In earlier days, we have to be very careful and cautious in applying the process of driving but later on it is taken charge by our subconscious mind. We start enjoying with friends and get engaged in some other activities while the vehicle is moving smoothly. So, we need to practice the skill so that it should be taken charge by our subconscious mind; it should be natural and automatic. Whatever we do, just develop an attitude to handover the activity to our subconscious mind, only then it becomes a natural and automatic activity.

1.08 REWARD AND PUNISHMENT

Fear and greed are the basic weaknesses of a human. When we see our activity carefully then we find that most of our activities are derived from our fear or our greed. In our society, many systems are being implemented to exploit this basic human weakness. Almost every organization uses the tactic of "reward and punishment" to make an employee to motivate them for higher performances. They also threaten them to punish if their performance is not up to the desired level. This reward and punishment method is used mostly for exploitation of an employee. It doesn't mean that this method is always harmful. Many people enhance their performance only due to their fear or greed. There are a various types of reward and punishment which are being used by employers and other agencies.

REWARD	PUNISHMENT
Promotion to higher grade	Demotion to lower grade
Choice posting	Punishment posting
Monetary benefit	Monetary loss
High reputation in society	Bad reputation in society
Reward and facilitation	Punishment

Our whole activities can be broadly categorized into two parts.

1. Derived by our fear or greed
2. Derived by our passion, our pleasure

The majority of the people's works are derived by their fear for punishment or by their greed to get something. If our driving force is our fear and our greed, then we are working under the pressure of some external bodies.

Actually it is just like an external pressure under which we do anything. This work is not self-driven but it is driven by some other person or things. Yes, a mass of people are working under this situation. And the most important thing is they even don't know about other driving force which may be better mindset and working experience.

There are just a few people who don't work under the pressure of greed or fear which is given by someone else. These people work for their own pleasure. When we work under the compulsion of our greed or by our fear then actually we are working for someone else. We are making happy someone else. Of course, we may be getting something but the fact is we are working for someone else. When we are doing something of other person then in most cases it will not be a pleasant act. It doesn't mean that to do for someone else is always an unpleasant work. To work for someone else is really a pleasing work if you love the particular person so much.

My simple view is to work under the compulsion is not always bad, since it also gives development and pleasure. But the quality of work driven by our passion is always very high.

When we work which is most suited to our passion then it gives great satisfaction apart from many things like better performance, better growth.

If you want to be happy for a day, go on picnic.

If you want to be happy for one week, go on a tour.

If you want to be happy for one month, go on vacation.

If you want to be happy for one year, get married, but

If you want to be happy forever develop an attitude to love your work.

– Unknown

It is very important for our children to develop their proficiency in a particular area in which they like to do most. If a boy chooses a particular field, then his involvement and growth will be great. But it doesn't happen always. The major incidence is just reverse to this. Majority of the people go to a particular field in which they have less interest. The saddest thing is it is not possible to give up the present job. It is not possible to switch over his present profession. Then what is the solution?

Option 1. Continue the present job for remaining service length up to his age of retirement with same mindset and attitude. His reaming life becomes very boring just like a burden. He accepts mentally there is no alternative way, and he just keeps on doing his job mechanically. Most of the people believe that they can't do anything else to their present job. This is just like a mental blockage that nothing can be changed in the present scenario.

Option 2. If his profession is not so suitable to his passion then the other option is to develop an interest in his job. He can find out a particular area in his job which he likes most. When we develop our proficiency in that particular work, our achievement rate increases and it becomes joyful. This is a very important method by which we can make our job joyful. This technique can be used in any area of our work to make it joyful. There are a large number of people who have learned the technique of taking interest in our assigned job. The rest of his reaming life becomes joyful.

Option 3. When, we are in such a job which we don't like and we want to switch over to another job, while switching is not easy. Then what is the solution? Just a few people will be able to think to switch over their present job after the age of thirty, forty or after fifty. It seems almost impossible to switch over after later years. But still a few people think such a way and switches over their job at the age of thirty, forty or even after fifty. How they could do? They do their present job 10:00 AM to 5:00 PM and start to work on his dream project in the time of 5:00 PM to 10:00 PM, as his secondary job. As his focus and involvement are mostly involved in his secondary job, it grows rapidly and fund flow starts from his secondary job. As the fund flow grows up, his action and involvement increases day by day. Later on his fund flow becomes stable and regular. He then decides to switch over to his new dream work.

1.09 WHY PEOPLE ARE SO GOAL ORIENTED?

Basic theory: "I am the best"

To understand the theory we have to go to ancient time, right from that thousands of games had played all over the world. Do you know why the games were played and till now it is played in a large scale. Some may say it gives pleasure, some says it is played since it is played since ancient time. But real inner desire for game is different. It is an event which makes a winner that "He is the best." This feeling develops in the mind of player. Football game is much popular in the whole world and madness of the football game is known to everybody. Just imagine that the goal post is removed from the play ground and all of sudden what will happen among the players and thousands of audience. All of a sudden, player will get confused what to do? The huge audience will not be able to think what they should do now? Without the goalpost, where they will strike? How they will judge who the winner is? When it is not clear that who will be the winner, the whole charm and enthusiasm will vanish in a moment. The basic requirement to prove that "I am the best" will not be fulfilled. Immediately, the charm of the game will vanish.

In this psychological desire, there are two components which makes the cycle complete.

- Performer
- Audience

Both the component complements each other. Audience motivates performer to perform very high. The presence of audience and their excitement and acknowledgement motivates the player to perform higher. Almost every person of this world thinks that his county is the best in the world. Why same type of thinking is found in all the people all around the world. Basically, it is motivated by the feeling of "I am the best." To support this feeling and to make him prove true, he puts all the positive things and hides all the wrong things. When the same person goes to other country and if he got the citizenship of that country he starts to praise that country. Actually he is trying to justify his decision, and in this process he puts forward all the positive things and hides all the negative things.

Now we discuss how this feeling of I am the best, helps in all type of development and growth. At the same time, all types of conflicts, struggles and wars are also caused by this feel.

Just enjoy the act of gardening: your garden will expand day by day. Don't think when my garden will grow in such a way that such and such things will happen. Don't think like this. This kind of thinking will lead you in the future, and you will start living in the future, and you will lose the pleasure of the present. You will lose the pleasure of process which is going on in present. If live in future immediately the present work becomes dull. If you lose your interest in job the quality goes down immediately since your involvement decreases in the activity. Then it is difficult to do it for a long time.

When we lose our interest, involvement of our mind and heart decreases, the act becomes monotonous. In this situation, the work is done half-heartedly and the quality decreases.

Any work which we have no interest is a type of punishment. Since our mind and heart doesn't take interest and situation compelled us to do that. A mental conflict arises and we lose much energy while quality and quantity decrease drastically, and we get tired very soon.

Our involvement to any work increases the quality of work. This involvement becomes an act of pleasure, and we keep on doing the job and don't feel tiredness. Now the question is why our mind goes in the future and we lose interest in the present job. The reason behind it is our goal-oriented mindset. We have been taught right from our childhood by our parents, by teachers and many different books how to set a goal and how to achieve it?

The whole problem arises from our orientation of goal-setting mindset which was taught from childhood. At childhood we were unable to question whether it is right or wrong thing. Till now we are unable to understand whether this goal orientation causes frustration and dissatisfaction in our life. I don't mean goal setting is wrong and useless. At the same time, I want to clarify that goal can be achieved in a better way if we just change a bit the orientation of our thinking. Of course, goal is very important but we have to think in such a way that we can enjoy our work too. I mean destination which gives us motivation and direction to reach our goal is important, but our journey should also be an enjoying thing. Just remember the life of Thomas Edison who invented a number of things which made the human life easy. Mr Edison used to work in his laboratory nearly twenty hours. Just imagine how a man could do so much work for so long period. By this fact, we conclude that Edison was not working for long hours but he was enjoying his work in his laboratory daily.

Our pleasure for any work provides energy and motivation for continuous work without exhaustion. A very interesting statement of Mr Narendra Modi, Prime minister of India, in a meeting is "I never dream to be something in life, I always dreamed to do something in my life." It is really a very big thing. It indicates his approach towards the task. It indicates that he is saying about the enjoyment of act. This approach of enjoyment makes him so energetic even at this age. Even young people not are able to match their energy level to Modi's energy level.

I want to explain the phenomenon by an example of a journey for any desired place of destination. I was going to Shimla with my family on a tour provided by my department. I have to start my journey from my home town Bokaro Steel City and my last destination was Rohtang pass. On the way, we have planned to visit many cities and many tourist places. In this real tour event if we all are keep on thinking only about the destination then the journey would be filled of anxiety we will think only about the last destination. In this mental setup the whole journey will be boring and a mental eagerness will ruin the whole journey. Since on the route we have to visit many places and all were new for all of us, we never worried about reaching our final destination. We were enjoying every place and every moment of the journey. Since every moment was new and filled with excitement we don't notice how we reached to our final destination. In fact we felt we reached very soon and now we have to start for return journey to home. By this incident, I want to just explain that when our attitude is to enjoy the process then it becomes a very pleasant thing and we don't realize how much time passed without our notice.

My view is to develop such mindsets which enjoy the process. He has no eagerness for his goal but he is eager to keep the process more enjoyable.

EFFICIENCY ORIENTED	GOAL ORIENTED
It gives pleasure every moment	It gives pleasure at the time of achievement
Keep us in present	Keep us in futures
Much involvement action	Involvement only in future goal
Process becomes joyful	Process becomes painful
Focus on your efficiency Enjoy the increasing of your efficiency Achievement is the shadow of efficiency	

1.10 CHILDREN ARE INBORN FUN LOVING

Go to any nursery school, and observe the general behaviour of children and it is very interesting to see how human is born as a fun-loving creature. Children have an inherited tendency to change their every activity into a fun, into a game. When a school bag is in their hand then they use the bags as a toy. If a few children are waiting for school bus they utilize this period and start playing even in a small period of time. Every time they make the moment as a fun. When children hear a school bell, they run to their home, throw their school bag and reaches to street to play with their friends. Parents worry about their food since they don't pay attention towards it because of their passion towards game.

My simple view is that we are inherited with fun loving, but gradually this approach of fun decreases and seriousness increases in our behaviour towards every activity of life. When our approach of pleasure decreases then our activity becomes a boring work. But what is the reason, why our approach changes and becomes so serious. In fact, we gradually become very calculative, and start to think in terms of money and other benefits. Thinking in terms of money has polluted our all normal activities. The development of such mindset has made our life very formal and joyless. Just remember how we used to go to our friends house and spent several hours without having specific purpose. Today our approach has accumulated money. We have lost our inner pleasure with our friends and relatives. All the relations have become very formal, and formal relation doesn't give real pleasure. It is just like a flower of paper which is looking more beautiful having no fragrance.

Nowadays people are not concerned to stand by with their friends in the event of joy. They want their friends only to expose their power, position and money. Many times they show how big contacts they have.

A person has organized a huge celebration for his child at its first birthday. Actually, he had acquired huge money recently in a land deal and he was very eager to show his earning to his friends and relatives. This is a fact that the person has got huge money recently; he will make his friends and relative depressed by describing and by showing his money in different ways.

There was a huge arrangement in which most of the renowned personality have been invited. The pandal was big; decoration and flooding arrangement was reflecting how money has been spent to make the party grand. It was very difficult to talk with the guest due to the loud musical DJ program. Happy birthday wish has been announced on behalf of the visitors. In this deafening noise, the one-year child was very much frightened and was crying continuously, but the child's parents had no care about their frightened child since they were busy in displaying their luxuries by the grand party to their friends and relatives.

The grand party was not the indication of love towards their child, but it is just a fabricated occasion to display their luxuries which they had earned recently. Be careful, specially, with those friends who are newly rich. They will not miss any opportunity to show that how rich they are.

Nowadays, the present modern life is passing through a very strange situation. Friendship and relations are secondary and money is the primary goal. We have neglected human relationship because of money. That is why we have acquired huge money but lost our friends and relatives. We have made us aloof from friends and society. The present thinking considers these things just as wastage of time. But it is very sad. When we realize the importance of human relationship, it becomes too late and we legged behind alone.

1.11 HIGHLIGHTS OF THIS CHAPTER

1. Survival instinct and pleasure instinct are two basic needs of human
2. "I am the best"—when one proves himself, he feels great and happy. The person who couldn't prove that "he is the best" in any way feels frustrated throughout his life
3. Expansion gives pleasure
4. Whatever we do are for pleasure or to avoid pain
5. Pain and pleasure are just our approach to see anything
6. Action, learning, achievement and pleasure are the four factors that make any activity joyful and make us involved in any particular activity
7. If you are not enjoying your work, you should not do that work
8. Most of the organizations use the technique of reward and punishment for enhancing the performance of employee. But they miss the basic instinct of pleasure
9. Fun loving is gifted to us by birth. But we have made even our game a serious thing

2. Passion and Strong Reason

2.01 GOOGLE FOUNDER HAD NO BANK ACCOUNT TO ENCASH $100,000

At first, there was no way to deposit the $100,000 check. It was made out to "Google Inc.," but there was no legal entity with that name. The check sat in Page's **desk drawer** for two weeks while he and Brin rushed to set up a corporation and locate other investors.

Google's passion and commitment are the prime factors, on which we have to work out achievements which are just the shadow of excellent work. The level of success of Google Inc. is beyond imaginations for anyone; even both the cofounder couldn't imagine such success. When it was started the average hit per day was 10,000 per day, and today it is 200 million hits per day. The growth is 20,000 times which is beyond imagination.

One very important aspect of great success we see in the working style of both the founders. They were very frustrated with the available search engine at that time and they were deeply involved in searching for a powerful search engine which will retrieve fast and provide most accurate information to the users. Their passion was to search a search engine which will be greatly helpful for all the Internet users worldwide. Their concern was not limited for their own benefit only, but for the concern of the whole world.

2.02 KNOW YOUR PASSION

Why is it important to know our passion? Our passion is our inherited tendency what we like to do most. As per our Hindu myth our life doesn't end with the death. It is just the end of our present body and again next birth happens with new body. This concept is called rebirth. After death, the body ends but our desire and our tendencies all get transmitted to a new life. Our prime desire and tendency continue in new life with a new body. Specific tendency and speciality reflects in the thinking process of next life. Suppose, a person has spent his whole life with nature then his tendency in next birth will be inclined with nature. So choosing the activity towards nature will be more enjoying and comfortable.

There are lots of methods and techniques by which we can recall our events of our previous life. Many cases came in the news about the event in which a child had a very clear memory about his previous life where he was born and where he lived his previous life. He described all his family members and the place where he lived his previous life. My simple view about my passion is to find out the activity I have done in my previous life. If I continue that particular work I will be more comfortable and will be able to develop more competence. In addition to this, it will be more enjoyable for me. It will be just like a punishment if I have to do a work which I don't like to do.

But, in most cases any event or situation develops our interest in a particular thing or in particular area. Our environment where we spent our childhood and the events which we use to see during our childhood play a big role in deciding our passion. Any specific person whom we met in our childhood also helps to develop our interest in any particular area.

- The environment where we spent our childhood
- Any specific person whose personality or life style impacted us
- Any specific event which develops our interest in a particular area
- Our parents and association develop an interest in a particular area

In a tribe, a young girl was in love with a young and handsome boy named Anshuman. And she wanted to marry him. Another influential and powerful boy named Sukhpal was also fascinated by the beauty of the young girl and he wanted to marry her. But her father was not in favour of Sukhpal. Actually, he hated Sukhpal but due to some compulsion of tribe he couldn't deny to marry his daughter with him. As her father was the head of the tribe, he wants to take every step in the matter of his daughter's marriage so that no dispute arises. An occasion came when he has to declare his decision about his daughter's marriage. He finds out a very clever solution. His method of solution was very interesting and nobody can object against his decision since he had given both the aspirants equal opportunity to prove their candidature. He called both the young boys and his daughter and asked both the boys to pull the girl towards their direction simultaneously. Both the boys held her arms and started to pull in their direction. All the people were thinking that the Sukhpal will successfully pull the girl in his direction since he was stronger than the other Anshuman. People were shouting and cheering up the contestants. A miracle happened although Anshuman was weaker than

Sukhpal, he managed to pull his beloved against the strong Sukhpal. Sukhpal was stunned since he was dead sure about his success in this contest. People were amazed that how Anshuman won the contest in which physical strength was the key factor of success. Later people realized the actual reason; while both the young aspirants were making their full effort, the girl was also pulling herself towards Anshuman since she hated Sukhpal and was in love with Anshuman. The girl's and Anshuman's effort together became greater than the force of Sukhpal, and Anshuman succeeded. This is a story which clearly pictures how our efforts become powerful and much effective when our passion is also in the desire. The girl represents just like our passion, and our passion combined with anything makes it very powerful. When we subtract our passion with any activity, the intensity and effectiveness decreases.

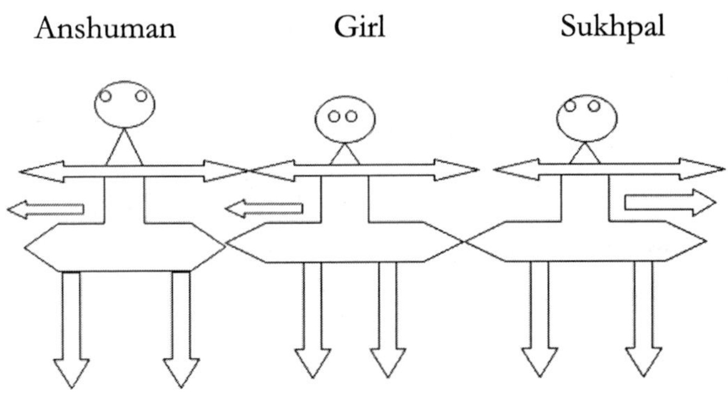

Our passion is nothing but it is our inner desire to do anything. Passion devotes our full involvement in any desired work.

2.03 PASSION, REASON, VISION AND ACTION

Suppose a big stone is kept in the middle of a field. Four ropes are tied with the stone, and four boys are pulling the stone in four different directions. Although, they are putting their full strength, they could move the stone hardly a few feet. It is obvious that the force applying in opposite direction were neutralizing the resulting effect. After long efforts they again sat down and discussed what the real problem was and why so much effort was not giving their desired output. And they found out that their effort in opposite direction was the real cause for the problem. Then they started to pull the stone in one direction and it moved easily with very low efforts.

Our life is just like the stone which is being pulled in four different directions. That's the reason why we couldn't make development in our life up to our desired level and why we devote our whole life and all our energy and time. The basic reason is clear that our inner agencies are contributing a great role in building our life and in the development of our life working in different directions. They are neutralizing the resulting effect. The four agencies of human mind are our:

1. Passion
2. Reason
3. Vision
4. Action

A man is working in an office in any department, while his inner desire is to be a journalist. He couldn't go in journalism. Here his output will not be up to the performance level as a journalist since journalism is his passion.

He has a burning desire to keep himself in touch with the day to day activities of state. But as his office job doesn't satisfy his reason of job, his enthusiasm level will decrease and simultaneously his performance level will also decrease accordingly.

He has a vision in his mind that he will be in touch with the high and influential people as a journalist, but in office job there is no such chances to fulfil his vision.

He wants to work as a journalist because huge movement and meeting different people are his desires. But, he has to deal with files sitting in the office. He never thought to do a work like this.

In this example, his passion, reason, vision and action always worked in different directions and the resulting effect was small. Despite hard work, improvements and enthusiasm were not up to the desired level.

Is there any solution for this problem? The only solution of this problem is to align all these in one direction. It is a fact that our response to any activity depends on how we feel, while we do? How we feel depends on what we think, and how we think?

2.04 HOW A BOY BECAME SAILOR TO A DOCTOR

A poor boy was sailing a boat at a lake and was earning money to support his poor parents. One day a young girl came to his boat and asked him for boating. During boating, she talked with the young sailor about his education and was very surprised that he was not capable for his schooling. She decided to help the poor boy and suggested to come to her home. She told him that her father will teach him for matriculation examination. He does accordingly and he passed his matriculation examination. Then she suggested him to prepare for medical entrance in which his father will help him. Her suggestion and guidance made the boy so much focused and determined. He applied for entrance examination. Due to the guidance and the help in studies by her father, he cleared the entrance exam and got admission in a reputed medical college, and he started his medical course. He was so much passionate about the completion of his medical course. He never thought anything else except his courses. He decided to dedicate his achievement to the girl. And the day, the moment, came when he got final certificate of his MBBS degree. He ran to his native place to dedicate his success to the girl, but he was shocked to know that she had passed away three months back. He was unable to understand how he was receiving her letters on weekly basis. He rushed to her father and knew that she was suffering from cancer. He came to know from the nursing staff who was writing letter on behalf of the girl, since she don't want to let him know about her cancer at this stage, as she believed that he will come back home to see her and not be able to finish his medical final exam. The nurse told him that, she made her to promise not to reveal to him about the letter, which was being written by her. Immediately the young fellow understands how much arrangements she had made to keep him focused on the exam and completion of the course. He felt dizzy and then he made vow to keep himself unmarried and devote his life to the service for the welfare of humanity and needy poor people.

Great learning can be derived from this real story.

- Strong reason is a prime factor for success

- Love has great motivation force which makes a man zero to hero
- Real love has only one desire to give more and more
- Helping other is really a divine feeling, and this feeling and pleasure can never be earned by money

Now analyse the story and find out the real cause of the success of the boy who was poor and had no goal in his life. Her guidance and suggestion made him absolutely focused to complete his medical course. A strong reason developed in his life to fulfil her dream to see him as a doctor. The level of passion and focus becomes very high which turned an average boy.

The basic problem is to make ourselves focused and passionate towards the goal.

- You must have a strong reason for goal
- Be passionate towards your goal
- Your passion will make you focused

Our mind changes frequently from one thing to another. This is quite natural state of mind. We may think something at one moment and other things at another moment. It goes to other things and again to third things. This is a very natural and normal state of human mind. But any event or any reason may cause to make our mind focus towards a goal. Any strong emotional thing helps to make our mind focused. The emotional things may be the following:

- Feeling of love
- Feeling of hate
- Feeling of humiliation
- Feeling of revenge
- Feeling of helping other

- Feeling of inferiority complex
- Feeling of superiority complex

All of these have very strong emotion which helps a man greatly to be focused. If anything happens in our life, that can be used for making a man focused for any great purpose in life.

If any of the emotions develops in the life of any individual, he becomes exceptionally focused and committed for his goal. These emotions have great power which makes a man focused and dedicated. Most of the films are based on the feeling of anger due to humiliation of hero of the movies. This humiliation makes a hero focused to take revenge against.

2.05 YOUR ACTIVITY BETWEEN 5:00 PM TO 10:00 PM

Everybody has to work at his work place for a certain time. Either he may work in a company or in the government or he may be a business man or may be a farmer who feeds the people of our country. So it is clear that everybody had to fix some hours for their livelihood. Let us take an average working hour that is 10:00 AM to 5:00 PM. We take this as everybody works for his livelihood during this time. However, the most important thing is what we do during 5:00 PM to 10:00 PM. This is a very important factor which decides your actual achievement of your life. The work which you do during 5:00 PM to 10:00 PM will change your life unbelievable.

What is your routine work during this period is capable to change your life. What is the activity of general people during this period? Most of the people just have their tea and supper in front of the TV set and watches the repeated news which is being telecasted by different channels in different ways. They make themselves involved in the talk show and analyse the pros and cons of the statement. Many become activist in their drawing room. On the analysis of our activity, we see that most of the time is wasted in front of the TV set. This is the story of an average person who is deeply concerned and talk about salary revision, salary allowance and retirement benefits. These are the most favourite areas about which they usually talk.

Just a few people who have some different vision in their life utilize this period. If he has interest in some higher degree, he joins a correspondence course and uses the time for his studies. Some has interest in share trading. He utilizes this time for that. The simple thing is these efforts make a big difference gradually in his life.

Some people have no reason and vision in their life. They spend their leisure time in watching and sleeping during the day. Now many organizations have started giving leaves on second and fourth Saturday. It is very painful since they have no desire and dream in their life. They pass the two full days in watching TV or sleeping the whole day.

If a person has no further desire and dream in his life and he passes his two days in watching TV and by sleeping the whole day. I feel they are just living a dead life.

2.06 HIGHLIGHTS OF THIS CHAPTER

1. Google founder Larry Page and Sergey Brin have great passion for a search engine for the Internet users. Their passion gave great things to the world which has changed the Internet world.

2. Identifying the passion and getting mastery in that particular field makes a man successful.
3. If you have strong reason in your life you will find the way of solution, or you may find an excuse why you have not done?
4. Your passion and strong reason makes you focused and then nothing is difficult in this world. An average man becomes successful due to focus and consistency and a talented man fails due to lack of focus and consistency.
5. An average man works during 10:00 AM to 5:00 PM and watches TV programs during 5:00 PM to 10:00 PM. But the talented persons are different in their life, and they work for their vision during 5:00 PM to 10:00 PM.

3. Power of Subconscious Mind

3.01WHAT IS SUBCONSCIOUS MIND

How to build positive habits? How to remove our negative and nagging habits? It is a well-known fact that solution of any problem depends on how correctly we understand the actual problem? Sumit is a well-educated person working in a highly reputed organization and earning good salary. But he has a problem; he just keeps on searching formulas and sutras which will change his whole activity and thought process. The second problem is he does not stick to any chosen formula.

Main problem: Unable to stick to a process and keeps on working on a particular thought.

Now I have to find that why he is unable to stick on a particular thought. Impatience is the basic cause of this problem. He wants the result very soon. But, he forgets that any creation takes time. Our impatient approach is the basic cause of failure and frustration.

Don't think about the result. The most important thing is to stick to a particular thought. Day after day, the thought will get engraved in our mind and it will start to change our life, our activity and our thinking process.

If we keep hold a particular thought, gradually it will establish in our mind and after some days it will change our life and daily activity. It becomes our automatic activity.

Why is it very difficult to come out from our old and nagging habits? It is difficult because we do not understand the process of formation of our habit. Without understanding the process completely, it is very difficult to come out from it.

Firstly we see the process required to form a habit

- Repeated action becomes a habit
- It is a gradual process
- It requires our attention, energy and time

There are a few examples which show how a repeated action for long time becomes our habit and later on becomes our automatic action.

- When we see an animal all of sudden in front of our vehicle, our leg automatically presses the break paddle
- When I park my vehicle, habitually first I ensure that no vehicle should be trapped due to my parking

Time, energy and focus

Wherever we pay it grows stronger. It develops on the following stages.

1. It becomes our habit
2. Then it becomes our automatic action
3. Compulsion
4. Mania

In a stage of mania, it becomes a disease. This stage is harmful and it requires some psychological treatment.

Now the question is how to come out from negative habits. Just remember that most of our habits have not been formed consciously. It has been developed automatically and unknowingly. I read a very famous quotation about our habit, "'We don't know how the habit formed' when we realized about formation of habit, then it is very difficult to break."

Don't be worried for removing negative habits; just stop paying attention, energy and time. The very interesting thing about these three things is they cannot be preserved for future use. If they are not used in a positive way it will unknowingly flow to the negative areas. It is just like an ice-cream either you test it or waste it; it will keep on melting and will finish by melting.

Very important fact is if we do not utilize our attention, energy and time for positive things, it will get wasted on negative things.

The level of success on our life is determined by how greatly we use our three great gifts given by God.

It is not the intelligence but the direction of intelligence makes a man successful or failed in his life.

Most of the parents are worried about the negative habits and activities of their children. They try their best to remove the negative pattern of behaviour. Basically the negative and unproductive activities are not the problem but indication of some problem. It indicates very clearly that positive activities are not so effective. In real science, two different types of activities can't survive simultaneously. This is not the right way to remove the negative activity. The actual effective method is something different, in which we make our focus on development of positive activity.

It is obvious that when negative activities expand positive activities will decrease, whereas when positive activities expand negative activities will decrease. The mass approach is to remove the negative activity for the balanced growth in life. Many times the direct approach doesn't work' while indirect approach works.

Second, the big mistake which most of us commit is we do not have patience to allow time to establish the positive habit in our life. We want immediate result and we get frustrated, when we don't get the desired result within a short span of time. It is a fact that establishment of any habit in our life takes time.

We should not bother for what big result I am getting, but the real thing is to continue the process. I want to clear it by an example of cultivation of a mango tree. My effort must be to protect the plant so that it should not be damaged by any animal. It must be watered provided manure time to time so that it must grow and keep alive. All of these activities do not give us mango fruits directly, but a situation is being formed in which the mango plant will give fruits as it grows completely. The conclusion is I can just provide the external situation in which the plant will grow, it will flourish and further it will give fruits.

Just in the same way any good habit we need to implant on our mind. We need to protect them and keep them alive in our mind. As the habit remains alive, it will grow day by day and after full growth it will start flourishing and will give fruits on many different manners.

Our prime objective is to keep any idea alive and active. Only then it will grow day by day.

3.02 HOW SUBCONSCIOUS MIND WORKS

The basic principle of our subconscious mind on which it works is our inner belief what we believe our subconscious mind produces accordingly. Our subconscious mind makes changes in our mind, body and behaviour according to our habitual thinking. It basically depends on few factors.

- What we think habitually
- What we feel habitually
- What we dream habitually

By the careful observation of the body of all type of animals and creatures we see how their body is changing according to their belief. A simple lizard changes its body's colour just by its strong feeling to hide itself from the insects and snakes especially for those who will eat it. To change his body colour, it feels very strongly to change its colour to hide and its colour changes accordingly. Its tongue is many times long in comparison to its body. It happens only due to its feeling to increase its tongue to catch insects from a certain distance. If the lizard goes much closer to the insects it will be alarmed and fly away.

Nature has given a very strong power of thinking and feeling. On this earth, millions of different species live. As per research it is an established fact that all the different lives are developed from single cell microbes. All the lives are living in different environment and their feeling and requirement to keep alive are different. And they change their mind and body most suitable to keep alive in a particular environment.

The greatest discovery of my generation is that people can alter their lives by altering their attitudes—William James

Our attitude is just the way we think and the way we act against any event which happens in our life. Our attitude is just like computer software which is loaded in a computer. The computer works according to the preloaded software.

Programs are just a set of instruction which makes a computer to do a particular work.

In human life, our right from our childhood, unknowingly a process of thinking and behaviour develops as and when any small or big thing happens. These collective experience forms an attitude towards life and towards any event. Basically this is just like software which controls our way of thinking and behaviour. In computer we change the software or upgrade the software for better or different performances. In human life also, the software is upgraded and changed. This is the reason why most of the aged persons' behaviours become very practical and polite. This maturity in behaviour is nothing but due to up gradation of the software in mind.

Up gradation of software is a very important thing which makes our computer capable in a more effective way. If we want to change our life we need to change our attitude and our behaviour. If our thinking and our attitude is as usual and we want something different in our life, then that is just foolishness. If we want to change our life the first thing which is required is changing our way of thinking and our attitude.

Many people complain that they are facing continuous failure in their business. They never realize that their attitude plays a vital role for a particular business. They require changing their frame of mind accordingly to best suit a particular business.

The biggest problem that lies in our attitude is that we don't want to change. Everybody wants his children and family to change. He wants his friends and relatives to change. He never feels or tries to change himself that is quite easy and practical; he never thinks to do that. The conflict and fight between people are growing day by day due to their mindset. Everybody wants other people to change.

Why most of the people are suffering with a feeling that they are right and others are wrong. Different perceptions are the basic cause of all of these conflicts. Every person is living with a very specific and unique perception which has been developed through a long and gradual process in his life. Every person has a general belief that he is living with the right perception. On the basis of his perception, he feels the difference in their perception and realizes that other is wrong. This is the point from where the entire problem arises.

Whatever we hold a perception in our mind, it produces several facts and logic in support of our perception. Actually our mind produces and finds the logic and facts to strengthen our belief. What we actually believe grows stronger day by day.

3.03 I CAN DO IT

We can divide the people broadly into two categories according to their thinking pattern. One person says I can do it. Another person says I cannot do it. These two statements reflect our thinking pattern and how it affects our pattern of thinking.

The first person says that I can do it then he switch on his mind in active mode to find out the possible solution. His activated mind finds out the solution. As we know, that whatever we say our whole mind finds out all the possible facts to prove the statement right. In this way, mind does many mental exercises to find out the probable solution. This type of personality keeps the mind in solution mode. To be in solution mode becomes his natural habit. Basic statement of these types of people is "It is difficult but can be done." This is the best example of positive people, who finds solution on every situation. They smile in every situation and always are thankful to everyone. In this pattern our mind keeps on thinking the possible solution round the clock.

So, the conclusion is either we put our mind in solutions mode or in problem mode. Solution mode sees solution in every problem whereas problem mode sees problem in every solution. Our repeated pattern of thinking and behaviour becomes our habitual thinking. Our subconscious mind accepts this fact as true and our thinking and behaviour change accordingly.

Now, we discuss the second category. He always thinks and talks he cannot do. People of this category switches off their mind against finding the possible solution. As he thinks he cannot do, he puts no effort to find the possible solution. The activity of his mind stopped due to his feeling about his inability to do that. His basic thinking is "It may be possible but very difficult." His pattern of usual thinking makes him fearful and makes him annoyed to everybody.

3.04 POSITIVE HABITS

Nothing is difficult

Nothing is easy

What is our habit that is easy?

What is not our habit that is difficult?

Everything is a matter of what we accept? Until then what we do not accept that appears very difficult and what we accept to do that becomes very easy. What we actually believe and what we actually accepted to our internal mind that changes our pattern of thinking and behaviour.

A poor man is poor since he has accepted that he will remain poor. A man is millionaire since he has accepted that he is millionaire. I see every day people are doing a very painful and hard labour for their livelihood. Actually, he has accepted that there is no alternative than this.

Our mental acceptance plays a very crucial role in deciding our destiny. This tendency heals us and also harms us. This mental acceptance makes our painful activity easy to bear. It decreases the intensity of the pain of any painful activity since our mind has accepted this as a reality. But it harms us when we accept it. Then, we lose our hope to something that comes out from the painful works. It eliminates our tendency to fight back against the odd situation through which we pass through daily.

Whatever changes that happen in our life start first with our way of thinking and way of our acceptance.

How to build positive habits? How to remove our negative and nagging habits? It is a well-known fact that solution of any problem depends on how correctly we understand the actual problem in detail. My problem is to just keep on searching one formula and sutras which will change my whole activity and thought process. And the second problem is not stick on any chosen formula.

Main problem: Unable to stick myself to one thought and keep on working on that particular thought.

Now I have to find that why I am unable to stick on a particular thought. Impatience is the basic cause of this problem. We want results very soon, but we forget that any creation takes time. Our impatient approach is the basic cause of failure and frustration.

Don't think of the results. The most important thing is to stick with these particular thoughts. Day after day, the thought will get engraved in our mind and it will start to change our life, our activity and our thinking process.

If we keep hold a particular thought, gradually it will stabilize in our mind and after some time it will change our life and daily activity. It will become our automatic activity.

Why is it very difficult to come out from our old and nagging habits? It looks difficult because we do not understand the process of habit formation. Without understanding the process completely, it is very difficult to come out of it.

Everyone has to cultivate disciplined and systematic life. It has to convey our subconscious mind through consistent practice and effort. Successful person makes the positive activities his natural activity which becomes his natural way of behaviour and action. Unsuccessful person unfortunately makes unproductive activities as his habit which becomes his natural pattern of behaviour.

Habit is just like a thin thread in the beginning. By regular activity, we add new threads every day and make it strong. Later on, it becomes so strong and it becomes very difficult to break it and come out of it. So, it is very important to care on the behaviour of a child. His repeated behaviour will become very strong day by day. Positive habit invites positive things and positive people in his life whereas negative things invite negative things and people in his life.

One person whom I know has very deep knowledge in the area of human body and how any disease develops in a human body and what is the best remedy of that particular disease. He has a great fond of hearing TV news and many informative talk shows which are usually arranged by most of the TV channels. In this process generally he used to go to bed after 11:30. That is why he is unable to get up early in the morning. Although he knows very well the great importance of morning walking for a sound health, he is unable to spare some time to go for a morning walk. I always feel that thoughts handle our process of thinking but our behaviour and regular activities are controlled by our habits. It is not so important how much you know good things, but the important thing is how much you have a capability to implement them in your life. Everybody knows that smoking is injurious to health; despite that many students and people smoke on a regular basis.

Firstly we see the process required to form a habit.

- Repeated action becomes a habit
- It is a gradual process
- It requires our attention, energy and time

There are a few examples which show how a repeated action for long time becomes our habit and later on becomes our automatic action.

- When we see an animal all of sudden, in front of our vehicle, our leg automatically presses the break paddle.
- When I park my vehicle, habitually first I ensure that no vehicle should be trapped due to my parking.

Attention, energy and time.

Wherever we pay it grows stronger. It develops on the following stages.

Very important fact is if we do not utilize our attention, energy and time for positive manner then it will get wasted on negative things.

The level of success on our life is determined by how greatly we use our three great gifts given by God.

We should not bother about the result we are getting, but the real thing is to continue the process. I want to clear it by an example of cultivation of a mango tree. My effort must be to protect the plant so that it should not be damaged by any animal. It must be watered provided manure time to time so that it must grow and be alive. All of these activities do not give us mango fruits directly, but a situation is being formed in which the mango plant will give fruits as it grows completely. The conclusion is I can just provide the external situation in which the plant will grow, it will flourish and further it will give fruits.

Just in the same way any good habit we need to implant on our mind. We need to protect them and keep them alive in our mind. As the habit will remain alive, it will grow day by day and after full growth it will start flourishing and will give fruits on many different manners.

Our prime objective is to keep any idea alive and active. Only then it will grow day by day.

3.05 AUTOSUGGESTION

Autosuggestion is a very popular tool by which we can convey any idea to our subconscious mind. To convey any idea to our subconscious mind is just like reprogramming our mind. We know that a particular type of person uses particular sets of vocabulary. For example, a depressed and frustrated person always talks that he is unlucky. He couldn't get chances in his life. Actually he does not know how he is using the very powerful tool, autosuggestion, against him.

3.06 HABIT LEADS YOUR LIFE

Knowledge is not so important if a person has no capacity to implement it into his life. And the knowledge is incomplete if we don't know the way to implement it in life.

A lot of books are available in the market. Some of them teach us to be successful in fifteen days. Some claims for twenty-one days, and some gives tips to make you successful in thirty days. Most of us often go through such books but no change appears in life. It doesn't mean that they are claiming wrong, but intense willpower and commitment doesn't possess all. That is why, it doesn't work.

Here, one thing all of us have to keep in mind is our pattern of thinking, pattern of our behaviour, and our perception that have established in our mind from childhood. For example, if my age is twenty-five years, then I have practiced the pattern for twenty-five years. The pattern established in our mind actually becomes our natural action. In the traits, which we have practiced for twenty-five years, some may be constructive and some may be destructive. All of a sudden, any traits cannot be absorbed or removed.

Any habit, either it is positive or negative, establishes in our mind gradually. Similarly its removal also happens gradually. Many constructive and destructive habits develop in our behaviour time to time. Initially we don't notice its formation, but we notice it later when it expands and affects our life.

It is a general belief that most of us are helpless against our old negative habits. Why is it very difficult to give up a negative habit? There are some wrong conceptions and wrong effects which make it difficult.

- Our panic approach for removal
- It requires a regular and persistent efforts
- Formation of positive habit (replacement method)
- Awareness required

Our habit is just like bondage of our life. This bondage becomes stronger day by day. It is difficult to give up a good habit if formed, and the same applies to our bad habits. Our habits are just like a plant which we water, manure and protect. It grows day by day and becomes stronger. When it grows bigger it requires less care, and it becomes very difficult to uproot the tree. It is good to form a good habit, since we do right things automatically. What to do if some bad habits have rooted in our mind? We pay attention to develop three things to make anything our habit.

- We pay focus
- We devote time
- We invest energy

Very simple fact is instilled then we keep on paying attention to these three things so that it grows day by day. But if we decrease these things to any activity, it dies gradually just like a plant. If we do not water a plant, we don't take care then it will die gradually. Twenty-four hours are available for everybody; if we invest this time in good activity then the negative habits will start to die day by day. If we pay our attention to positive activity, then we will not be able to pay our attention to negative activities and it will decrease gradually.

It is very important to struggle or fight against the negative and unproductive habits; no need to remove it by applying our will power. Rather we have to use here displacement method. Just replace the bad things with good things and bad things will remove automatically. It is fact that two things having opposite nature cannot survive simultaneously. Any real artist cannot go to do any work of destruction. His basic tendency is creation.

For a person who has great desire to just gain from other, it is very difficult to give something to others. His inner tendency is just to gain. A miser person just keeps his mind involved to make curtail and save it in his bank account. Generally, we may think that he is living in very crisis since he has no tendency to expand money. But his pleasure is concentrated in depositing his accumulated rupees in his bank account. He feels a great pain in spending money.

3.07 MASS HYPNOTISM

What is mass hypnotism? Mass hypnotism is a feeling of compulsion to do a particular activity which the mass people used to do by tradition. The people who are doing them are also not very clear about the main reason. They just learned it to do since a large number of people are doing. Subconsciously, we accept that "what a mass people are doing" is correct. It is just a normal belief that what huge people are accepting and doing are obviously correct.

The fact is that we are just copying the activities. It is interesting that when a child sees his father smoking, it gets fascinated with the activity of smoking. He feels that smoking is a very enjoying thing and also thinks that he becomes an authority person for the family. He doesn't know the adverse effect of smoking. He is only fascinated by seeing this act which is being done by the family head and many other people. This is just a very simple example how we adopt many unnecessary and harmful things in our life since many other people are doing so. The second interesting thing is that they had started these things by same way. This is the way by which a lot of unnecessary and harmful activities just keep on going from one generation to another generation.

Suppose you are going to a market and if you see many people gathered at a place and watching something, then automatically a curiosity will arise in your mind to see what is going on and what the people are watching there? The activity of mass people will attract you to watch the activity. Everybody has many habitual activities which may have started only due to curiosity and gradually have become normal habits.

People are learning positive and negative habits only by copying others. Most of the social and religious behaviours are being adopted by us only due to the effect of mass hypnotism. It means that we just keep doing what the mass people do.

A very interesting example was conducted with a group of monkeys. Five monkeys were kept near a ladder to reach a banana and there was such an arrangement that when a monkey climbs to the ladder cold water was spread over the other monkeys. As the cold water is spread, the monkeys started to hit the climbing monkey. Again a new monkey was brought and when it tried to climb the other monkeys started to beat the climbing monkey. Now a new monkey was added to the group who had not faced the cold water. But, as he saw the other monkeys beating one monkey, he joined the group without knowing why they are beating and started to beat the monkey who was trying to climb the ladder. This interesting phenomenon is also applicable to human beings. We just start to do many things which are done by mass people without knowing the actual reason. Most of our traditions are followed only due to the mass hypnotism. We just keep on doing the act without knowing the actual reason of doing such things. The reason for starting such a tradition may not exist now. We can understand the act of the monkey which started beating the monkey climbing on the ladder without any reason.

Unconsciously, we think that since so many large people are doing so, it is right and we must also do it. There is also a fact that mass compels other people to join in those activities what they used to do. This is based on the concept that everything expands itself for its survival.

Two forces work in this mass hypnotism.

- Individual is attracted to join the group.
- Mass compels an individual to join the group.

These two forces act as a very powerful compulsion which is called mass hypnotism. It is observed that an average person always goes with the mass without thinking rationally about the activity. But, there are very rare people who think rationally and check the relevance of the particular activity. They question about the relevance.

It is very common that traditional people don't like such questions, in fact, they have no answer. When anyone asks any question, they give some readymade answer like this:

- Questions should not be raised in such a matter
- It is our tradition
- It just happens like this from earlier
- You are younger to understand this
- By time you will be able to understand

The fact is he doesn't know the right reason. He never tried to know the answer. Those who ask such questions are treated as outlaw. The mass wants only those who accept the tradition without any such questions. Women were burnt at the funeral of her husband. This was a very old tradition and thousands of women had to die burning alive with her husband only due to the old tradition which can't be challenged at that time. Since this was just an old tradition, nobody could dare to oppose this tradition. But Raja Ram Mohan Roy opposed this cruel tradition when it happened in his own family. It requires a very strong will power and conviction for his belief. Finally, a movement started and it discontinued after a long struggle. Normally, an average person couldn't have strength to oppose the tradition and so much conviction for his belief.

This is just an example to show how many wrong traditions keep going on. Nowadays science and technology have developed and we are capable to see on the basis of scientific approach. Even now a number of traditions which have no scientific base are going on despite of that they continued as usual. Issue of child marriage is even now popular in many communities and in many areas although it has been declared illegal and punishable.

Why we don't want to give up the old tradition? People become comfortable with the old traditions. Moving with the mass people gives a feeling of security. If one opposes any tradition then he feels a threat that he may be boycotted by the society, which will invite a number of other problems including his security. This one is a very important aspect which makes people with the old and even wrong traditions.

Our area of thinking is mostly restricted by many things like our family, profession, our society where we grow, and the organization where we work. A guide said that his family is involved in the profession of guidance' since last four generations. It is very interesting which shows how many young men went to his traditional profession. Actually his traditional profession has restricted his thinking in that particular area. It is a normal behaviour that one feels fear to go or think something different. We want to live in a comfort zone.

In this world, all the mediocre people read and discuss history but just a few people who have strong reason and strong vision creates history. From ancient times, many things have been researched and discovered which have changed the way of thinking and the way of living.

3.08 HIGHLIGHTS OF THIS CHAPTER

1. Our impatient approach and lack of consistence are the key factors which make a man unsuccessful in his life.
2. Acceptance to any ideas or thoughts makes it easy and natural activity which plays a vital role in our success.
3. It is our habits which control our life not our thoughts. Successful people make positive activities as their

habits whereas unsuccessful people make unproductive activities as their habits.

4. Be careful and check whether our focus, energy and time are being utilized in productive activities or unproductive activities.
5. I can do it or I can't do it. First statement activates out mental activities whereas second statement deactivates our mental activities.
6. Noting is easy and nothing is difficult. Anything that is our habit is easy for us and anything that is not our habit is difficult for us.
7. The way we think, the way we deal anything that is just a matter of our habit. Positive habit upgrades our life whereas negative habit degrades our life.
8. Our acceptance is a very important factor which determines our life. A poor man is poor since subconsciously he has accepted that he is poor and will remain poor. A rich man is rich since he has accepted subconsciously that he is rich.
9. Autosuggestion is a self-talk technique by which we reprogram our subconscious mind for specific purpose. It is a process of impregnating our subconscious mind by a particular idea or thought.

4. Power of Belief

4.01 HOW WE ATTRACT ADVERSES IN OUR LIFE

Life up to the age of twenty years is believed that it is decided by our previous destiny but later on the life is just our own creation knowingly or unknowingly. It is obvious that our present life is the result of our activities five years back while our present activities determine our five years later life. Our dreams and our feeling attract the things required to fulfil our dreams. Dreaming is a very natural activity of human life. This is just a process of living a life which we actually want to live. If our future life keeps on displaying in our mind in the form of a day dream, then it becomes very powerful.

One of my school friend used to behave just like a sick and a very weak man usually even in his home. In year 2008, he suffered by a heart attack, latter on one day a road accident happened in which he was injured badly and he had to be bed ridden for five months. After that it took a long time for him to walk and to join duty. Even now, he is suffering due to that accident. My simple view is that if you act or feel like a sick man, then you are attracting such situation into your life. Our subconscious mind doesn't make any difference in actual desire or our feeling. It treats our feeling just as our desire and it produces the things like that.

Even our act starts happening in our life. At the age of 35, I used to walk just like a polio patient for making fun. My wife always used to warn me not to do so even for a fun. Suddenly, I realized a pain developing in my legs. My actual walk changed due to the pain which developed in my legs. Lastly, I had to undergo medical treatment. Everything became normal after two months. The doctor couldn't clarify the actual reason, but I realized that it was just because of me, my acting for fun. Then I realized that my subconscious mind didn't take my act as fun, it took it as my desire and arranged the situations accordingly.

If we see the life of great achievers, we can realize that they were dreaming their future life from their very early stages of life. I found in my life that early vision and early dreaming are the very powerful ways to attract anything in our life. It is just like an eclectic power, whether we know or don't know, we can get the benefit of electricity just by switching on a fan and can get a cool air from air cooler. It doesn't need a deep acknowledgement of electricity. In the same way, whether we know or don't know the power of feeling and dreaming, we are affected by it without fail. But if we know the working principle of our belief, then we will be able to use the power for achieving our dream and will be able to avoid the unwanted things.

What are the practical ways by which we can use these very powerful techniques in our life?

We can collect some pictures and literatures about our desired thing. These pictures help us for feeling and realization of the actual things which we desire. Actual feeling and realization are very helpful in attracting such things. We can visualize those situations and events which will take place when the event actually happens. For example how people are reacting and congratulating you. The most important and powerful process is acting just like it already happened. Our feeling and our action attracts our desired goal in a very powerful way. Suppose your friend asks you that you are looking sick then it will not be more effective. But, if any doctor asks you that you are sick then you will believe it since a doctor is an authentic man as per our belief and we will feel sick. The main purpose is to convince our subconscious mind. When it accepts then our body produces result on our body and our life according to that.

The key factor is how to convince our subconscious mind? It is just a technique. Any equipment can be fitted in a very easy way if it is fitted properly. Otherwise, we have to put a lot of effort and all will be in vain if we try in incorrect method. Similarly, if we adopt a right way then it is very easy to convince any idea to our subconscious mind otherwise it is very difficult. It is just like a growing a plant, we can't make it grow by force. It is just a slow and automatic process which takes place gradually. We just provide water and manures which are required for its right growth. However, we have to protect it from external agencies like goats and other animals.

Any idea is just like a plant which is slow in our subconscious mind. It grows gradually. We have to protect it from other external things which may damage the idea. We can provide only the situation in which it can grow in a balanced way. And the most important thing is when it grows up to a certain level it doesn't require such care and protection. At this stage, it is self-sufficient for own growth and survival.

A very simple concept is that we can't grow a plant by force, we just can irrigate and provide manure and protect it from outside agencies which may damage or kill the plant. Suppose a boy enjoys playing cricket then he will have to protect his desire to play cricket from the negative and destructive elements which may steal his dream by their negative view about the game. He must be away from those who are very fearful about the uncertainty in cricket as a career. They may make his confidence week. So, he has to protect his dream to be a cricketer from all such negative and fearful people. Secondly, he has to flow his attention and action always towards this game. This consistent flow of his attention and action will develop the root and makes it strong. Our consistent feeling and action gradually develops our acceptance in our inner mind. As the acceptance level increases, it starts happening in our life. Our acceptance makes anything actual in our life.

It is just like spreading the root in the ground. A plant spreads its root gradually in the ground and the plant grows stronger and stable. Spreading of the root takes time, but as it spreads to a bigger area the growth of the plant becomes fast.

Seeing and believing is the basic fundamental of our mind. We believe what we see. Our belief is our acceptance by subconscious mind. Our acceptance changes our mind and body accordingly.

4.02 RICH AND POOR MINDSET

A very latest report says that the 50% of wealth of the whole world is in the hand of only 62 persons of this world. And 99% of the whole wealth is in the hand of only 1%. Is this not a is strange fact and have you ever thought about this fact? There are lots of misconception about poverty and prosperity. The basic fact is just a mindset which makes a man rich and poor. It is a very good example of our internal belief. A rich man is rich since he has a mindset of rich man. Feeling of abundance attracts abundance in life. Poor people always think about scarcity and are filled with a fear of loss of money. His focus on loss and scarcity creates actual loss and scarcity as per the universal law of our belief.

A criminal always keep on thinking about crime which makes him a criminal. A rich man keeps on thinking about money and money only. His habitual thinking is revolving only around the money. His action, his feeling and his dream all are aligned to money only. The fact is what we deposit in our mind expands in our life day by day. Gradually thinking pattern revolves only around the money and no other feeling and activities are allowed in mind. His activity strengthens his feeling about money. Our actual feeling develops our life too.

Rich man has a passion to be rich. He has great love for money; this passion motivates him to do tremendous efforts to acquire money. In fact his activity for earning money becomes a fun due to his passion for money. His passion and fun make the business activity just like a game for him and he develops skills, right decision and investment in businesses which make him rich day by day. At later stage, the growth happens in compounding effect and so the rate of increase of the wealth increases rapidly.

A poor person always feels lack of money and will be fearful for the loss of money. His habitual feeling becomes his reality. He always hates the rich people. This is also a big blockage in his mind which stops the flow of money in his life. Poor people's mind is filled with a number of wrong perceptions which are responsible to keep him poor always.

- Earning money is a very tough job
- Rich people earns money by illegal means
- I am unlucky in concern of money earning
- I have no family support
- I have no skill for business
- Much money is sign

The wrong perception deposited in his mind keeps him always poor. Any changes will happen only when we change our perception towards money. But, changing the perception is not so easy although there are some basic things which can change one's perception.

Millionaires have some specific personality traits which make them an average man to millionaire. The traits which they have inherited and many they develop according to the need of their goal.

1. **Great vision:** Great performer of any field has many similarities, but the most common similarity is the "Vision." Millionaires have great vision in their life which is very strong and very clear. Clear vision always navigates person's thinking and performance which leads him to his big goal.
2. **Ability to take risk:** Risk-bearing capacity is a factor which differentiates them from poor mindset. This risk-bearing capacity comes from his strong vision and strong belief on his dream project. If a person does not have a strong confidence to his vision, he will not be able to take risk.

3. **Team building:** It is not necessary for billionaires to be very talented in their schooling, but they have great talent to hire talented people who can work for their dream day and night. So the hiring of talented people and making a cohesive team plays a vital role in creating a big corporate. It is very popular saying that it is not necessary to know everything but the important thing is to hire people who know everything of a particular thing.
4. **Selling skill:** Producing or manufacturing anything is not very much important but the most important thing is to sell the product. Selling is an art and it requires a great skill. Promotion and selling are both very crucial items for business growth.
5. **Goal setting and planning:** When a team works, then it has a pre-set goal and a strategy to achieve the goal. Setting of goal and its systematic achievement is monitored carefully so that the whole team puts their 100% contribution for the realization of the goal in a given time frame and in given resources. Best definition of our intelligence is to perform highest level in a given situation by the given resources.
6. **Passion and profession:** Millionaire really loves their love. In fact they know their passion very well and they devote their all resources in that particular work which he likes most to do. His passion becomes his profession. He doesn't work in his company but he enjoys his work at his office with his team.
7. **Product and service innovation:** Innovation is a prime factor which makes always demand in the market. H don't like to follow the beaten path, in spite he always creates new path through his innovative thinking and

innovative ideas. Any product and services remain in the market if it is being modified time to time as per the latest trend and demand which changes time to time.

Proper Planning Prevents Poor Performance.

4.03 CHANGE YOUR ASSOCIATION

Your perception regarding anything will be the outcome of your association and the environment where you grow and you live. Your company with poor people will make your wrong perception strong. You will not be able to question your perception since all are having the same mindset. So when you want to do something new in your life, first you have to change you perception. And your perception depends on your association, and that is why I ask to change your association.

In every country, millions of people start new business and they fail within one year. They don't understand that what the actual reason is. They could not develop the actual mind frame and the way of thinking and dealing what is required for that particular business. So it is advised that any young aspirants should first associate with some successful business person and get real live experience of business dealing on the cost of business man's profit and loss. After getting real live experience with the association will help to develop the way of thinking, the way of dealing and the mindset most suitable for the particular business. Later on, he should start his own enterprises. Then the chances of failure will be a minimum.

"In early stage learn the business dealing with a businessman, on his profit and loss, after experience start your own venture"

One very important thing is to invest on your development. In India, we are very hesitant towards investment for our development specially after getting a comfortable job. Basically, poor mindset people are always fearful on any occasion of expenses of money. He does not realize that this is an investment. For any big venture, initial investment is essential. Fear of loss of money always prevents him to do any investment of any type. Investment is a primary thing for any business concern. The investment may be in the form of many types, like

- Investment of money
- Investment of time
- Investment in building good reputation
- Investment in expansion of idea or business

All of these are kinds of investment, which gives great returns in future in different ways. A person of poor mindset people is very afraid for spending money. He plays too much safe game. The person who is too much cautious, never achieve something great in life. Over cautious represents a fearful mind. Fearful mind couldn't grow broadly. It develops negative approach and finds always negative things in any work.

Your focus develops anything you are focusing. If a person keeps on thinking and talking about his health problem, he is expanding his health problem. A person always think and talk about business loss and failure, he expands failure and loss in his life.

Our mind never differentiates between constructive and destructive thinking. It just responds according to the pattern of our habitual thinking. Our fearful thinking pattern attracts many negative things in our life.

4.04 HARD WORK OR SMART WORK

My father always suggests me to work hard. His core belief is hard work which is the only tested formula that makes one's life successful. He also keeps on doing hard work every day since he never feel that there must be some other way. I realized right from my childhood despite his hard work his standard of living and life style never enhanced. I don't mean the standard of life style means a luxurious life. I mean, the standard of life means a comfort and peace in mind and in life. He must have sufficient time for relaxing and time to do some work which he likes to do only for fun.

My view about real standard life is just a bit different. Picture of a real happy life differs from man to man and it shows what our prime focus in life is?

- Capable to do what you like to do
- Enough time for what you like to do
- You have a circle of core likeminded people
- There must be some creative work in life

It is my definition about a real successful life. But it doesn't mean it will be acceptable to all. I never realized that I will also like the life style of my father. I also differ from his "Hard working concept for success" it doesn't mean I dislike hard work. But I want to modify it to make it interesting. If we make our work interesting, then it doesn't seem hard. Hard work sounds just like an effort of labour class effort. All knows that labour class exerts most hard work while his life is very hard work. Hard work clearly indicates that a work is done without having interest in that. That is why I don't like to do hard work, but always advocate to make any work enjoyable. To make any work enjoyable is an art and we become skilful it we have an approach to make it just a fun. Labour class people work but they are paid very less. That's why the life of a labour is very tough all around the world.

I always intended to make our job joyful. It can be termed as smart work rather than hard work. My emphasis is on smart work, since this approach increases our productivity and the quality of work.

For example, we can travel from Mumbai to Goa by many travel means: By road, by train, by air and by ship. Apart from these popular ways, there are several other means which make us capable to travel the distance. But the question is the best and smart way of travel this distance. We have to choose a smart way to travel this distance. It depends on the basis of the cost we pay, the time we invest, and the energy we invest in the process. Smart work and hard work both are just a mindset, the way of our thinking process. Smart performer always keeps on thinking about the method of work by which he can enhance his productivity. To increase his productivity he has a tendency to learn the process more and to enhance the process gradually. In fact he doesn't like to just keep on following the beaten path. Innovation in thinking and in working always reflects. He never feels hesitation to move on the new path. Of course he fails many times but he never bothers for that since he believes very strongly that committing mistake is a part of learning. But the person who believes about hard work, he always goes on the tested method. He never wants to take risk of any type.

If a carpenter works for eight hours per day then he devotes at least one hour in making sharpen his instrument.

Many people may think that this is just wastage of time. But they don't know that this investment of one hour increases his productivity. So, the smart performer always pays attention in developing his skill which develops his productivity where as a hard worker has no interest in learning the skills for the development of his work.

The other very important difference is a smart worker enjoys his work, since his rate of achieving is very high which makes him very motivated and enthusiastic. Hard worker doesn't feel so much enthusiastic since the rate of success is very slow and his work becomes very dull.

4.05 WINNERS VERSES LOSERS

A piece of paper flies in the air by the mercy of the air and according to the air, whereas a kite flies in the air by its ability to fly in the air. An aeroplane faces a lot of resistance during flying in the air. But it has been designed in such a way that the air creates a lift to the plane to fly in the air. So the message is that our challenges can be converted to an opportunity if we have a burning desire to keep flying in the air.

It is just a common phenomenon that everybody wants to be successful. But at the same time everybody doesn't want to face the challenges. Challenges and difficulties act just like a filter that filters the winners from the gathering of average people. We don't like challenges but challenges are the real factor which identifies the winners and makes a man a winner.

Winners	**Losers**
Likes challenges, faces the challenges	Don't like challenges and escape from the challenges
I will do it now	I will do it later
Always learns new things to enhance his performance	He has no interest to learn new things
I will create opportunity	I couldn't get opportunity
He takes responsibility	He escapes from responsibility
Usual statement "Yes, I can do it" Usual statement "No, I cannot do it"	
Tendency to fight with situation	Tendency to flight from situation
Always finds solution	Always finds an excuse

Have you ever realized how our process of thinking and our environments are correlated to each other's? Our pattern of thinking changes our external situations and external situations changes our inner thinking. When our will power is weaker than the external situations, the external situations control our life. But when our internal will power is stronger, it controls the external situations. When an employee joins in any organization then he is quite junior and he has to act just according to the instruction of higher officers. But gradually, when he gets promotion and rises to the apex level, the whole systems run according to his instructions At the starting level he was just a part of the system and now he is the director of the system.

In any organization a man is just a part of the system, he keeps himself remain just a part of the system or he may develop himself as a boss of the system and the system will run according to his desire. The conclusion is very important.

"Either you control the system or you will be controlled by the system"

In a forest there is one very popular law that is "Either you kill the other animal or the other will kill you" for our life we can take it as "Either we should have control over our external situation or external situation will have control over us."

In any organization we can work just like a part of the system or you may be the controller of the system. You may be just like a passenger of a vehicle or you may develop your skill and ability and put yourself on the driving seat. Then you will be able to drive the vehicle in your desired direction at desired speed. Most of the people spend their life just like a floating log in a river and they move according to the flow of the river; they have no any desire or strength to move in their own direction. But just a few people have a very strong dream and strong will power that doesn't live according to the system requirements but they are capable enough to give and run the system according to their dream and desire.

My very simple view is that all of the things are just a matter concerned to our will power. How strong is our will power. When a person claims that the situation is very difficult, it doesn't mean that actually the situation is difficult. The fact is that his will power and skill for dealing the situation is weak. When our skill and ability develops, we handle the difficult situation very easily.

People see that how Sachin Tendulkar had hooked a ball very easily for six runs. He may think the ball was so easy, the fact is different. He had practiced so long and developed mastery in such shots that looks very easy. Our skill and efficiency make any situation very easy. Lack in skill and efficiency makes any situation very difficult. Our tendency is to blame other things. We never say that is inefficient, instead we say the situation is difficult.

See the process of learning of children. He crosses many stages in the process of learning to walk and run. First a child used to see every person who is walking and running around him. This environment develops a strong desire in his mind to walk. He crosses many stages in the process of walking and running. What actually he learns in the process of learning to walking. He learns to make himself balance against the gravitational forces. In this process, he falls many times and again he gets up and makes other efforts without any hesitation and frustration. His strong feeling and confidence compels him to make several efforts to make him stand against gravitational forces. It mainly practices the skill to make balance with gravitation.

A child first tries to move on its two hands and two legs. Later on he makes himself capable to sit then he tries to make him stand up with the help of any support. After that he learns to keep him stand up without any support. After making him capable stand up without any support, he tries to move a few steps and he falls in the process of moving ahead. Again he stands up and again tries to move. He fails many times and ultimately he moves a few steps. This regular effort becomes successful after a few days. Everyone has a good experience and shouts when he moves on his own feet.

This complete process shows how a child keeps on making effort to make him stand up and capable to move and ultimately how he succeeds in his great desire.

A child learns the skills to keep him standing and then running is by the trial and error method. He doesn't learn it by reading a theory book. This is a very interesting thing that nobody reads the theory part of balancing, but all learns it by practice. Riding a cycle is not learned by reading a book or by learning how to ride a cycle. It is just learned by regular practice and by trial and error method.

Like standing of children and leering of cycling is not learned by reading but it is learned by practice. To keep our mood happy and make it always positive attitude is not a matter of study but it is learned by regular practice. This is a very interesting thing that most of us read many books and articles about positive thinking and positive approach. But we don't realize that it needs practice. Study doesn't help more. Most of the times more study puts many concepts in our mind which makes us confuse what to do and the process becomes more difficult. More thinking about different process several times make a man incapable to take any action.

We find a lot of things which require only our consistent practice but we just keep on doing research work on these things and the real purpose to adopt the skill in our life gets defeated completely.

a. Positive thinking and positive behaviour
b. To be focused on your goal
c. To be cool, consistent and disciplined
d. To avoid time wastage activities
e. To enjoy our work and activity

These are just a sample list to illustrate how these activates are not the matter of studies but it requires regular practice just like cycle riding.

Everyone feels that many things are very difficult to adopt in life, and many things are difficult to give up. Every one of us has passed this process to make him stand up and to make him walk on his feet. When we grow as a young man we may feel hesitated to make so intense effort to learn any skill. Suppose I have a tendency to be angry when any unwanted thing happens and I realize that such angriness is not good and I should have to change myself. Our way of dealing can be changed completely if I can make consistent effort just like a baby.

What is the problem, why we are not able to do so consistent efforts like our child stage? The reason is very interesting. At the stage of childhood we were not concerned about what people will think if I couldn't succeed. There are many reasons which make us unable to make consistent efforts like a child.

- Fear of failure
- Fear of people's reactions
- Lack in strong desire to do
- Low confidence level
- Our old tendency resist the new activity

4.06 STORY OF A FROG

Many frogs were living in a well. Due to some reason the water of well became poisonous. As they realize that the water is poisoned and it is difficult to survive, all started to make efforts to come out form the well. People gathered on the well and started to shout that "you can't come out from the well, you can't do." It was interesting many were trying to come out but they fell into the well. They were making efforts to come out, and the shouting of the people "you can't do" disturbs their efforts and they fall down into the water again. Among all the failures one frog was climbing consistently despite to all the shouting that "You can't do." It was unaffected of the huge shouting of the people, and it was climbing firmly. At last it succeeded to make him come out from the poisonous water.

People were cheering the frog on its grand success since it was just a matter survival. And same time all others failed to come out from the well. But the large cheering and huge sound didn't make any more response from him, and then only people realized that the frog was dumb. Then only secret of his success came out to the public. Actually the negative shouting that "you can't do" not affected the frog since it was dumb while other frogs accepted the negative comment given by the huge crowd.

So, the moral of the story is very simple "Just be dumb like the frog." If we pay attention to the negative comments of general people then our confidence level and commitment towards our goal will decrease, and it will make us fail. Average person are very concerned about others comments. If we are affected from other's negative comments, then it proves that our confidence level and commitment level are very low.

Smart and handsome people don't bother for other's negative or positive comments on their dressing scene. Their inner confidence is so strong about their personality; they don't care for such comments. But when a person is not so smart and handsome then he gets disturbed by the negative comments about his dressing sense.

4.07 RAMKRISHNA PARAMHANS

This is a very remarkable story of Ram Krishna Paramhans which shows how an imagination backed with strong feeling changes our mind and body. As we know that Ram Krishna Paramhans had practiced the many ways of worship towards God and had shown to the world that all the paths are just the different ways to reach a single God. Apart from many worship methods, he worshiped God through a specific method "*Sakhi sampraday*" in which every member worships God Sri Krishna by considering himself as the wife of God Sri Krishna. Even the male member assumes himself as the wife of Sri Krishna.

In this process of specific worship, Sri Ram Krishna felt like he is a female and he is the wife of Sri Krishna. He was so deeply involved in this worship. His feeling and realization was so strong. Gradually his voice became just like a lady tone. His walk changed. His disciple felt embarrassed when they noticed many physical changes in his body, for example, his breast started to develop like a women. His movement gradually changed just as the movement of a woman. His disciples made a joint request to him to stop this worship method and then Sri Ram Krishna stopped this worship. It took almost six months for him to become normal as he was before this worship.

This is a very true incident in the life of Sri Ram Krishna which shows how we can change our mind and our body by our imagination with a deep feeling. So it is very clear that what we dream and what we feel that actually we become.

Biologically human are classified as masculine or feminine. It doesn't mean that any man is 100% masculine or any female is 100% feminine. As per the research, man and woman are classified by the quality of masculine and feminine. A man means he may have 75% masculine characteristic and 25% feminine characteristics. A woman means she has 75% feminine characteristics and 25% masculine characteristics. This ratio changes person to person. In many cases the percentage lies on a very margin difference like 49% and 51% or it may be 48% and 52%. When such a marginal difference lies, then the event of sex change happens. Very often, we used to hear such news that by a surgical operation sex has been changed.

The characteristics of masculine and feminine are the qualities which can be increased or decreased by our feeling and by the different training. Here, my simple conclusion is that when our imagination and deep feeling change our sex which is generally believed that is made by the almighty God, then why can't we change our destiny? Why can't we make ourselves poor to rich? Why can't we make ourselves dull to smart?

Nothing is difficult. Only it is difficult to accept. It is difficult to believe that anything can be done. In our nearby we see that many people have acquired a huge money by all the means. It doesn't mean that they are very talented and those who are poor are not talented but of course there is a difference between them. The difference is their imagination and feeling towards money. Those who acquired a huge money has one speciality that is they love money very much. They have only one thought, only one vision in their mind and that is abundance of money. This vision and great feeling of love for money makes them rich.

On the other hand poor people are filled with a fear of losing money which keeps them poor always.

What is our usual imagination? Are we enjoying our imagination? It is just like a two-way effect. Our achievement gives us confidence. And our confidence increases our achievements. One thing boosts the other. When we enjoy our imagination then our achievement increases, while our achievement increases our imagination becomes more joyful.

There is a centre point in a circle. Our thinking and feelings are just like a centre point and our external life and achievements are just like circumferences which are developed from the centre. Whatever changes we make to the centre point, ultimately it gets reflected to the external areas. Our core belief controls our whole life. What is our core value? That is very important since our whole life develops and revolves around our core values. If our core values are constructive then constructive things will grow in our life, and when our core values are destructive then destructive activities will develop in our life. So the important thing is to work on the core value which expands to the external sphere of our life.

We can take an example of a school. All the activities and curriculum activities are governed by the vision and guideline issued by the principal. By any way if we change the mind of the principal, the whole activities will be changed accordingly. If the working style of the principal is not good, then the whole activities of the school derail. Whereas the disciplined and strict approach of principal makes the whole school disciplined.

The internal changes in our thinking change our external life. And our external life changes our inner pattern of thinking. Effect happens always from both sides.

Wave in a pond always expands to outward. We apply a force at a point in a pond and this force expands in a circular form in all the directions. Wave is nothing but it is expansion and transfer of energy from one point to another point.

4.08 HIGHLIGHTS OF THIS CHAPTER

1. Our habitual thinking of adverse situation attracts such situation in our life. If we visualize unknowingly negative things, then it will happen in our life. The same process applies for positive thing also in exact same way.
2. Your perception makes you capable or in capable.
3. It a great fact that the life of successful people is filled with many failure. Average people don't dare to take risk and has no capacity to start a new venture.
4. Committing mistake is part of learning. That is why a winner never fears for mistake or failure. Since either you win or you learn.
5. Your perception develops from your parents, association and the book which you use to read.
6. Your association makes your approach towards life positive or negative.
7. The world is filled with people who work very hard. Merely hard work is not enough; it must be smart also, which gives better and bigger results.
8. Average people don't like challenges but winners like it since it filters the winners from the collection of average

mass people. Challenges provide an opportunity to sharpen our skill and ability.

9. An aeroplane has to face a huge resistance due to air. But it has been designed in such a way that the same air creates a lift force to aero plane by which it becomes capable to fly in the air.
10. If our belief and commitment to our goal is strong then comments from other people will not be able to stop us reaching the goal. That is why people having strong belief and commitment become dumb against the comments of average people.
11. Our internal feeling and belief even changes our sex. Then it is obvious that anything can be changed in our life by our thinking and belief.

5. Focus Your Goal

5.01 STUDENT LIFE: THE BASE OF LIFE

Technology has made our life very easy and comfortable, but we don't notice how this technology has stolen many things from our life? We don't realize the adverse effect of the over use of these technology. Addiction is always used for bad sense. Our new generation is now addicted to technology. These addictions are grabbing our life gradually and many are on the path of spoiling and many had spoiled life. Understanding right and wrong things usually don't develop in teenage. When they understand these negative effects, they are fully grabbed in the addiction of technology. At this stage, it is very difficult to come out from these things.

Student life is the golden period of life. But, any student doesn't feel how people say that it is a golden period? This is just a four-way road, where we have liberty to go in any direction. The fact is we feel the importance of things when it passes away from our life. The childhood of present time is not as joyful as earlier thirty years back. Seriousness of life has grasped our new generation from its very early stage. I ask my son to go out and meet his friends, but it seems that he has no much interest in these activities.

Technology has given us a number of equipment which makes our life very convenient and joyful but the saddest thing is the pleasure in meeting people is lost. It is true that communication connected us so much; we feel that the whole world have become a global village, in which people are so connected like they are living in a village. But there is another side of technology which is very dark. We don't know the people who are living beside in our building. We are connected with a large number of people, who are living far distance from us, and we communicate with them very often in a day through what's app and face book but we don't know who our neighbour is.

Let us see how collective meeting of people decreases as technology made many things easily available in our life. Think about the time before popularizing the TV sets. We have only just a few things for our entertainment like cinema hall and theatres where live plays were performed. The theatres were not so available in small cities and other than meteors. Only the cinema was the most popular means of entertainment where 3–4 shows keep on going on a regular basis. People used to go to cinema with friends or with their family members on a particular show at a particular time. There was no option to see picture at their convenience of time. The time was fixed and mass people go there for watching cinema. Today, technology has made a movie show so convenient that we can see picture on our TV at our convenience of time at our convenient place. Now it is not required to gather a huge people at a particular place at a particular time. This technological development minimizes the opportunity to meet people and see the picture at one place. Now small theatre is available in every house. People need not go out for seeing picture.

Earlier, meeting friends and people were the biggest source of entertainment and time pass. Today, a number of options are available for entertainment and time pass like

TV channels, mobile and DVD, and the most interesting thing is these are available anywhere anytime basis. The most interesting thing is the mobile which lies in our pockets always. Which chatter all of our needs?

Earlier, people used to meet each other mostly for their entertainment and time pass. But nowadays these things are fulfilled by our electronic devices.

5.02 THANKFUL AND GRATITUDE

Negative events and negative emotions are more effective to our life in comparison to the positive events. Most of the people have many complains in their life, and they always condemn God that God has not given them happiness, wealth and many other things. Many of them feel that God has made injustice to them. Over all, people used to think and complain for what they lack in their life. Very few people realize that whatever he has got in his life has been created by him only. In general, people have the tendency to take responsibility for what is going good in their life, and blames the other for their failure in life. It indicates how our escaping tendency denies our responsibility. By many events and examples it has become an established fact that our complaining nature increases the opportunity to complain. Actually our unhappy feeling about our life becomes a cause to create more unhappy moment and things. Our complaining nature radiates our unhappy feeling. The universe treats this as we are sending signals to invite the unhappy things.

The universe only responds according to waves which are generated by our feelings. It doesn't distinguish between right and wrong signals; it just responds our mind wave according to its nature. Right and wrong is just our definition. Nature doesn't discriminate in right and wrong thoughts.

If unwanted events and unwanted things come in our life it clearly indicates that we are sending such mind waves by consistent thinking and feeling. We can reverse this process by the direction of our thinking in positive way.

To be thankful and feeling gratitude are two very powerful tools which make our feeling positive and create very powerful signals to the universe. This can be understood by our daily life phenomenon. Suppose any person has gifted me a very useful book to me which helped me a lot in my profession, and then what is my responsibility to do for his help. Quite naturally, I should be thankful and feel gratitude for his help. When I feel thankful and feel gratitude to him then he feels that he has helped a right person. When we don't show thankfulness and gratitude, then he will feel that he has helped a wrong man who doesn't deserve such help. Actually he will realize that he has helped a non-deserving person, and he will stop such help further. But for a thankful person, he will realize that he has helped a real deserving man and he will help him whenever he needs help.

Our thankful and gratitude feel for what we have received in life creates a very strong wave which attracts such things in our life. Our feeling attracts very strongly for which we feel thankfulness and gratitude. But those things we condemn and criticize will go away from our life.

We need to develop an attitude of thankfulness and gratitude for every single thing we receive in our life. Suppose we develop a thankful attitude for our wealth, then our wealth will be attracted in our life by several means.

Not only our wealth, we should not condemn the wealth of others too. If we criticize the wealth of others, then our wealth will also be taken away by many means.

The very simple process is to be thankful for everything which we have received in our life. Thankfulness must develop in our natural way of thinking and behaviour. Most of us have developed mastery in condemning everything in our life. We have to reverse the process. It is just a skill to see and realize some positive things in our live for any situation or any events.

PRACTICE TO BE THANKFUL AND GRATEFUL

When we start the practice to be thankful and grateful, it will appear very funny. But later on it will be our natural way of thinking about the positive aspect of everything of our life. When it becomes our natural way of thinking then only it will start reflecting in our life.

A very famous psychologist Gestalt had shown a very interesting picture of two faces facing each other. When we see constantly on the faces suddenly the two faces will disappear and wine glass appears. You will be surprised to see how the two faces disappeared and a wine glass appeared. As you will start to think about the two faces then again it will appear in the picture but now the wine glass will disappear. Then you will realize that when you see the two faces, you can't see the glass, and when you see the glass the two faces will disappear. This experiment shows a very important aspect of human mind. In our thoughts, two things may exist but at a time we can see only one thing.

GESTALT PICTURE

Now, how is it true in our life? Suppose I perceive that Manoj is a very good boy then I will see his good aspects only. Even I will have a tendency to take his negative aspects as good. For any reason, if my perception changes due to any reason, then I will take even his positive quality in a negative way. This is the way how human mind perceives anything and takes anything.

5.03 MANY LOVE MARRIAGE FAIL

When a boy and girl come in contact and fall in love with each other, they treat their lover as the most ideal person in this world. In this stage, both are in such a fantasy world where they see everything as most beautiful things in the world. In such fantasy mind frame, they see every positive and negative thing just as positive qualities. But those who are not in such fantasy mind frame at that time they judge the positive and negative aspects in a balanced manner. This is the reason why a parent fails to convince their children about the negative aspects of their friend. The fact is just like a hypnotic mental state where logic and fact creates any effect on the youth.

This is just an illustration how our mind takes any things. When we see the positive things then we don't see the negative things, and while we see the negative things then we don't think about the positive aspects. When we have a mental belief that "I am an unlucky man," then everything will certify that I am really unlucky. We will not be able to see the good things in our life. And this way, day by day situation and events will take place in such a way that will make our belief very strong that "really I am very unlucky." But when we start to think that "I am very lucky" then every events and situation will appear in such a way that will convince that "really I am very lucky."

All these examples prove that when we start to see the good things then the tendency to see and to feel the bad things gradually gets eliminated. But if we have a tendency to see the negative things then it is very difficult to see the positive things in our life.

Everybody is living in a prison made by him.

We expect appreciation from everybody but we do not appreciate anyone. This is a basic contradiction in our habit.

We want to be wealthy but we don't appreciate the wealthy person.

We want love in our life while we condemn the act of love.

We want to be successful in our life but we don't accept other's success.

We want care from others, but we don't want to care others.

We want respect from others but we don't want to respect others.

We want many things in our life while we are not thankful for what we have already received.

These are some basic mistakes which keep on going in our life day to day. And we blame that how many unwanted things happen in our life. In fact, these unwanted things indicate that there is something wrong in our habitual thinking pattern. It is necessary to make changes in our pattern of thinking if we want to change the unwanted things in our life.

5.04 CHANNELIZE YOUR ENERGY TO ONE AREA

"It is not the talent which makes a man successful in his life, but the direction of his talent makes a man successful in his life"

It is very important that talent plays a vital role in making a man successful in his life. But the talent itself is not enough for success. Our energy and effort are needed to be focused then only it creates. Every year many million gallons of water falls in the form of water from the sky and it is drained to sea through different rivers. Hardly a few percentage of the rain water is used for constructive purpose on the earth. As we know, flowing to the lower level is the tendency of water, and the flow leads the water towards the sea. Our lakes, ponds and river just hold very small percentages of the rainwater, which is used by all the living things of our earth.

By construction of a dam, we stop the natural flow of water; it is used for irrigation and hydroelectricity generation. When we make a reservoir and store all the unused flow of water and channelize its flow, it generates huge amount of electricity and provides irrigation facility to our agriculture and fulfils the need of water the whole year. If the water is simply allowed to flow, then it will be drained to the sea without any notice.

Majority of people waste their energy just like the rain water flow. They don't care how their energy is being used; in fact, it is wasted in unnecessary activities. Therefore, majority of people are unable to do any useful achievement in their life. It doesn't mean that there is lack in their talent, but of course, there is lack in focus and priority. Most of our intellect and talent are wasted in unnecessary activity, since we have no focus in our life. Water has a natural tendency to flow downward; this is a universal fact. A very strong dam is required to stop this unnecessary wastage of water. This dam not only prevents wastage of water by preventing unnecessary flow but it channelizes its flow for generation of electricity and irrigation. Similarly our energy has a natural tendency to flow out through many activities which are mostly unproductive. Basically we are wasting our energy and talent mostly in unproductive works. Just like a strong dam, it requires to prevent all our unproductive use of our energy and to channelize it for productive works. In human life, what does a strong dam mean? It means anything which makes our energy to channelize in one direction and prevent all the unproductive use of our energy. It is not so easy since we have to work against the natural flow of our energy and our tendency.

This is the point where most of the people fail to preserve their energy for the productive use. It requires great will power or great motivation. Our great poet, Kalidas, has created Ramcharitramans the great holy book of Hindus. He was just like an ordinary man who had great passion for his newly married wife. But after an incident his focus completely turned 180 degrees. His life changed completely, he devoted himself completely in the devotion of Lord Rama and wrote Ramcharitramanas. What happened by this particular event was his wife had scolded him for so much passion. This particular event stopped all his unproductive use of his energy and channelized in the devotion of Lord Rama.

Today our students are facing a great problem that is "unable to make them focused."

I found this fact in my practical life from many examples of success story of an average man who attained success only due to his focused and consistent effort. Many examples are available in which a talented boy failed in his life only due to lack in focus on any goal.

5.05 HOW TO FOCUS?

1. Must have a clear vision
2. Must have a strong reason
3. Must have a strong belief

In the earlier chapter, I had discussed how our achievement becomes a great motivation factor. In our daily life, we see that everybody is focused in some particular activity. The activity may be productive or not. Today, it is very common that children are wasting their most valuable time and energy in video game which is available in laptop or mobile. It is a fact that if he is not enjoying a productive work then he will involve himself in unproductive work since it is a human inherited nature.

Achievement and pleasure are deeply correlated to each other. Since pleasure is a basic need of human, he keeps on searching for some achievement from either productive work or unproductive work.

We can broadly classify our pleasure into two categories on the basis of what we get.

- ✦ Positive pleasure
- ✦ Negative pleasure

Apart from our productive and unproductive works we also derive our pleasure from other people by making them happy or unhappy. It depends on our mind frame whether it is constructive or destructive. Every day we see that a large number of people are involved in doing something great for the betterment of other people which give them plenty of satisfaction and pleasure. On the other hand, a large number of people are involved in making some problems in the life of other people. Both are doing a work for their own pleasure. It basically comes from our inherited tendency which is acquired right from our childhood.

Now we understand how both the positive and negative happiness differ from each other. It is a natural law like an eco-sound, what we speak loudly returns back to us in the form of an eco-sound. When people give happiness to others, it returns back to them in many ways. Similarly, when we give pain to others it returns back to us in many ways. In our day to day life, we see it and realize it in many ways for both positive and negative pleasure.

When a person realizes this pleasure of giving others, he keeps on thinking how to enhance his capability to give pleasure to more and more people. These desires compel him to form a team or company which chatters his desire to give pleasure to more people all over the world. World's companies have been setup to help the other person who returns the founder immense happiness and pleasure.

This is not only true for good things but apply for bad things in same way. Those people who are habitual for negative pleasure they form a team to enhance their capability to give pain to others. Actually they form a gang. Our negative behaviour for pleasure returns back to us many times bigger. Everyone knows how the dictators of the world died. These are nothing but the returns of their dictatorship approach.

Creation of happiness works just like a chain reaction among the people. The speed and intensity increases in geometry progression that is why it is very powerful.

5.06 HIGHLIGHTS OF THIS CHAPTER

1. Addiction to anything is harmful. Technology has made our life very easy and comfortable. At the same time, it had stolen many things from our life like peace of mind and physical exercise and causes many physical and mental diseases in human life.
2. Where we focus that expands in our life. If we think about frustration and pain more, then frustration and pain will increase in our life. Thankful and gratitude

are two very powerful tools which attract thankful and gratitude moments in our life.

3. We see any person according to our perception, and form an opinion according to our perceptions. But most of the time our perceptions are very different from the actual quality of that particular person.
4. An average man becomes successful by his ability to make himself focused and consistent towards his desired goal. While most of the even talented man fails only due to his lack in focus and consistency towards his coveted goal.
5. Clear vision, strong reason and strong belief make a man focused to a particular goal. It is just like a skill and ability which can be developed by regular practice.

6. Dream and Destiny

6.01 DIFFERENCE BETWEEN MAN AND ANIMAL

Have you ever imagined that a lot of similarities are found between human and animals? They live their life which has a lot of similarity with human life. Somebody can say that animal has no intelligence power and no creative power. But the researches have proved that they have intelligence and they have creative power in many areas even more than a human being. This question is very interesting and its answer is also very interesting. The one thing which is the basic difference is the capability of "Imagination."

Dreaming is a basic factor which is not found in animals. Many cannot believe it, but we can realize this fact in our day to day life. We see that a butcher keeps dozens of goats at a place and everyday he picks up a goat and slaughter in front of all the goats. Despite the act of slaughter in front of them, they don't feel that they will also be slaughtered at someday. They live their life in a very comfortable manner. This happens only due to the lack of the power of imagination and dreaming. They don't imagine that they will also be slaughtered someday. This lack of imagination power keeps them very comfortable even if they see everyday goats are being slaughtered. They can't imagine that this can happen to him. They live comfortable even if everyday goats are being slaughtered.

So, imagination power is a great gift which has been given to human. All of the great researches and creations we see in the world happened only due to the imagination power of human. Whatever we see in our life, they have been created in our mind first by the power of our imagination. A huge apartment is constructed, but this is first created in our mind by the power of imagination.

Whatever happens in our life first appears in our mind by the power of our imagination. But we also misuse power of our imagination for wrong pattern of thinking. For example, many times we worry about some miss happening, and due to consistent imagination we attract unwanted events in our life. This is just an example, how we utilize our imagination in negative way. Human has created paradise on this earth only by his power of imagination and also made hell on this earth only by his power of imagination.

We were comparing between man and animals. But between human there is also big difference in the power of imagination. Our imagination power makes a man creative and constructive. Even among human a few people have great imagination power while most have almost negligible imagination power; these people are very close to animal with two legs and two hands.

Our imagination, visualization and feeling are great tools which fabricates our way of thinking and way of behaviour. For example, when we visualize any dangerous situation many symptoms start to reflect on mind and body. Our actual feeling and imagination gradually attract things to our life. Capability and incapability are just our mental feeling and our mind and body changes accordingly.

Our imagination power and visualization play a vital role in creation of our destiny. So, if we want to change our destiny, first we have to change our imagination what we use to visualize.

Our process of thinking is by creation of visuals in mind. Our visualization is a mental activity which is based on the actual things or on actual events. For example, we see an orchard of mango fruits, and all the plants are small now. Now we imagine how this orchard will be visible after five years. Here our visualization is based on the present situation. The process of visualization happens on the basis of real object which is visible now and which we can touch. Then we imagine its future look and status on the basis of our past experience and we project a picture on the screen of our mind. It can be formulated as

Real object + past experiences + imagination power = projection of future image (visualization)

This visualization is a projection of anything after passing some times in terms of weeks, months or years.

Second way of visualization is the combination of two different things and creation of a new third object in vision.

A horse is an animal which walks and runs on earth.

Bird is a creature which flies in the sky.

Both the two facts are combined and a third creature is created by the combination of the two actual lives. We visualize such a horse which have wings like a bird and the horse is capable to fly in the sky and also capable to run on the earth. This is a very simple example of a visualization in which a new thing is created on the basis of actual objects.

How visualization and our imagination become powerful and how we can use it for creation of our desired destiny?

In the previous example, we discussed that imagination is a mental process in which we imagine something which will develop in future on the basis of its present state. For any imagination, we must have some base on which our imagination develops. Without any base our imagination will not be more effective. Now we understand how it makes our imagination powerful and effective, which fabricates our desire and destiny.

Assume that I want to purchase a brand new car. There are many problems like finance and some other family responsibilities. I can use my power of imagination for removing the problems and achieve my coveted car.

- I collect information about my desired car and coloured booklet of my dream car. These information and broachers will help to visualize and feel about the car. This feeling will help for the removal of the entire financial and other problem.
- I can take test drive of my dream car, and the driving experience will create a very strong feeling of car, which will remove all the obstacles and car will be in my portico within few months. Actual feeling of driving experience creates a very lively feeling about the car. The lively visualization and feeling become very effective in realization of our dream car.

Whenever you visualize anything, a wave is generated which travels worldwide. Our mind actually works like a transmission station which creates waves by thinking any particular thing and we also receive waves transmitted by other person. All of us have some experience about this. Sometime it happens. You may think about your friend and he may knock your door, and when you open your door you get surprised to see him and say that I was just thinking about you. This is a very common experience which most of the people have realized at many occasions in their life. The reason is very simple, when your friend is coming to your home obviously he is thinking about you and a picture is running in his mind. This picture is transmitted all around. Since this wave is related to you, your mind receives it and you start to think about him. Here, your friends mind is transmitting waves and you are receiving the waves.

When you keep a particular picture in mind then a particular wave will be transmitted regularly, which is received by the people who are related to such thoughts.

I have experienced it frequently in my life. Since I have a transferable job, I always used to search such house, which has a big garden. I found a house for rent which had very big garden. What you are searching for there are the people who are also available who want to offer such a house for rent. Your subconscious mind always finds miraculous solution for your inner desire.

You can attract anything in your life by persistent visualization. You can make your visualization power powerful and effective.

- By persistent particular thinking
- To associate such people who also think the same thing
- Regular feeling as it has already achieved

Association of people, who have same vision, makes the particular imagination very strong and it sends very strong waves, which attract people very strongly.

Mahatma Gandhi had a big vision to make our country free from British. His strong vision collected the likeminded people with him. Gradually the large number of people associated with him and it converted in a great movement for freedom, as we know whole country associated due to the law of exponential growth. It happens just like a chain reaction.

Anna Hazare movement, a recent event, is also a best example of how a strong vision converts into a great movement just like a chain reaction. The fact is initially Anna associated a few very honest and dedicated people in his movement. This association of 5–6 people attracted nearly 30–40 people. These 30–40 people attracted 200–300 people. These 200–300 people attracted 2,000–2,500 people. This way a mass people associated with him and it is converted into a mass movement. This shows how a strong vision attracts a few people which later changes into a mass movement like a chain reaction. Vision of one man became the vision of millions of people. In fact, this movement associated all those people who had a feeling of pain in their mind due to corruption and those who had a strong desire to make our country corruption free India.

6.02 DREAM AND MY DESTINY

My friend has a very popular saying that success is a matter of luck, labour and chance. I feel that, the factor which makes a man successful is very clear in his mind since he is confident about this. In this statement one point is labour which is in my hand and the two factors:

(1) Luck and (2) Chance are not in our hands and are not in our control. It means success is not in our hands. This is also an example of perception. Another interesting thing is he is dead sure and he accepts nothing other than this thing is correct. This is also an example of a particular vocabulary of a particular person. It is very interesting to see that a certain type of people uses a particular set of words while others use another set of words. First I will list down some popular sets of words which generally failed and people often uses.

- I didn't get a chance
- My luck is not favouring
- I couldn't get my family's support or father's support
- I have no powerful connection.

By the analysis of the statement we realize a very important tendency which makes others responsible for their failure. This indicates a very poor mental attitude to escape from own responsibility. This type of people will always blame others for failure and take own responsibility for any achievement. Very interesting thing is to have eagerness to take responsibility even he has really no credit for that particular activity. He will blame others even for his own mistake.

Some people have the tendency to take credit even for those things which has not been done by them, and blaming others even for those things they are responsible. This particular behaviour is now very common in any organization and in any assignment that is being done in a team. Another very popular wrong tendency is to express our own work in a very big way and the work of other person in a small way.

Every year, thousands of religious organization happens are all over the world. Thousand and even millions of the people take part in such organization. Those people are so fanatic and passionate towards these organizations. Many fatal accidents happened and many people lost their lives in such organization. These huge gathering are basically motivated by fear and greed. They are so mad and fanatic. These people think that if they couldn't attend the gathering then they will lose very big things in their lives and will be deprived from the grace of God. This strong desire and panic behaviour cause a big miss happening.

This is just a perception. To be part of such religious activity is an act of great fulfilment of their life in many areas. They bear all the adverse and pay all the cost in the form of physical pain, time, energy and money.

A very interesting line I found: poor beggars are begging outside of the temple and the rich beggars are begging inside the temple.

Nobody has real love to God. Every person has some personal needs which can be classified as follows:

a. Success
b. Prosperity
c. Health
d. Pleasure
e. Own job or children job
f. Marriage of children

Here is an important life event of Vivekananda. He was passing through very economical condition, Then Ram Krishna told him to pray to Maa Kali for the solution of his economical need. He went in front of the statue of Maa Kali, he prayed but couldn't ask for money but he asked only wisdom. Ram Krishna sent him again to Maa Kali, again he asked for wisdom not for money. All the three times he prayed for wisdom only but he couldn't pray for the solution of his economical need.

All people must think of the desire in their prayer to God. Is it not power, position, money, better education for children or their health issue? Nobody prays for wisdom. All are just praying for degree and best placement. An average person's prayer is mostly related to these areas. Wisdom and devotion are very exceptional need of exceptional people. Basically our thinking and behaviour are rotating only around the power, position and money.

Wisdom and moral value has lost its importance in the perception of modern people. People are fearful that if they live an honest life then they will behind in the flow of modern life. Many of us feel that now moral education is wastage of time. In a programme where top rank students had being awarded for their excellent performance in competitive examination, one reporter asked which one is your most favourite subject and which subject you dislike most? A girl replied that physics is her most favourite subject while moral education is just wastage of time. I was stunned on her response. Our modern thinking is so concentrated on materialistic things like highest package and comforts of life, it even don't realize the need of the moral education and moral values. This is just an example about how low importance is being given to moral values. Its effects are observed everywhere in our daily life.

Everyday law and order problem arises. Scam and fraud are normal features of present life. People are brutally killed, many unwanted events happen even in a market and nobody does anything. There are a number of incidents which are increasing day by day. Deterioration in moral values is the prime cause of such incidence. Many people advocate that this is the problem due to weakness in law and their implementation. Otherwise, all will be solved. But it is a fact that punishment is not the solution of such situation. Otherwise after impression for few years, a criminal should become a man of value. But it doesn't happen so. Basically it is the matter of mindset, which creates problem due to their pattern of thinking and low moral values.

Everyone blames that new generation has very low moral value which is the cause of problem in society. But the question is who has taught him right moral? Children are receiving moral from the following way.

- From parent
- From school
- From society where he grows
- From books and their association

PARENTS: Parents are the first teacher and home is the first school of every human, from whom children get moral education. In most of the case children get moral education from their parents, who have contributed great for the human. But in modern days priority has shift in 180 degrees angle. The most dangerous thing is parents have no own moral values. How can they give moral values to their children? Secondly many parents think that if his children live his life with high moral then he will lag behind in this competitive life. So, he internally doesn't give much weight age to such value. And the result is happening every day. How illegally a student acquires question sets and involves in many unwanted works from his very early stage in school. We are blaming young generation but the fact is they couldn't get right value education from their parents.

SCHOOL: Now see the prime focus and way of education of almost all schools. It is very obvious that to make a student a great human being is not their priority. To make him a man of high moral values is not their priority. The only priority is to make the students to score highest and highlight their school in the city, state or even in the country. It is just like a business concern in which increasing profit every year is the prime focus. To create very high competitive environment is just a tool for attracting more brilliant students who will pay more high admission fees and miscellaneous charges. Many highlighted schools display the top performers in their school display which attracts more meritorious students and those who are capable to pay high fees and miscellaneous requirements.

In any business concern, profit making and profit increasing are prime focus around which all strategy and workflow are designed. Our schooling is also working in the same style and strategy. Concern towards moral education is not in priority. So this channel which is a very powerful channel is involved in developing the mindset of earning money only.

Most of the people are shouting that law and order must be strengthened to check the crime in society. But nobody is concerned about the children growing with low moral values which cause many type of crime in their later age.

Many people have a very strong belief that power in hand makes a man corrupt. But the fact is not like this.

Actually power in the hands of a dishonest person is harmful to society and for nation. Power in the hands of an honest person is a boon for society and country. But power makes a man corrupt is not correct. How we think and our perception about corruption is bit wrong. In any office a clerk bribes 100rupees and a politician bribes 100,000rupees and our perception says that the politician is the big corrupt. But the fact is both are same in corruption. Since a clerk has limited power he has bribed only 100 rupees. If he becomes so powerful like a politician where he may be paid huge amount then immediately he will enhance his bribe like a politician.

SOCIETY: Our children where they live they don't see any great personality or any high-valued people. They see only corrupt politician, businessman and bureaucrat. They couldn't see any ideal personality in their locality to make him their ideal. Today, people of high moral values are not available easily.

The people who have no moral values in their life today hold most of the high and powerful posts. Their position and power are very attractive to the younger generation. The young generation is at immature stage and they are not capable to discriminate the right and wrong things on the basis of a long run effect. They just observe their attractive position in society, and unknowingly they make such person their role model. This way our younger generation are choosing the wrong path which later becomes a problem for the society and country. It is very sad that corrupt politicians and bureaucrats become the role model of our younger generation.

In this situation the person having high moral values faces many difficulties since the majority has no values in their life. Lower category people having lower values are keeping themselves in lime light of society and high-valued people feels neglected and keep them away from the main stream since it is occupied by third grade of people. So the society is dominated and lead by the third grade people who have acquired power and position by unethical means. They have only one priority in their life that is to earn name, fame and power at any means so that they can exploit our society and our country.

Today most of the parents are less concerned about the value their son is receiving but their concern is focused on the grade in examination on which his power, position and package will be decided. His efforts fulfilled and he got best placement with a very high salary package. Now, his son pays his parents everything in terms of money and all the comfort which can be purchased by money but doesn't like to spend his time with his parents.

A very successful student got a job in the United States and was paid very handsome salary package. He shifted to the United States, after sometime he was informed that his father's leg fractured in an accident. He asked him how much money you need for the best treatment just inform me I will send it through Internet. But his father says I don't need money, however I want you here in this painful situation. He replies that "I can't do this." His father now desires only the presence of his son at this juncture of time but his son has no time for him. What happened?

Actually parents have emphasized always on good grades, best placement and highest position. They never taught him the importance to the human relationship. As his son reached at the age of four he got admitted to a very famous boarding school. He always grew in an environment where he lived the formal relation where everything is being paid in terms of money. He never realizes the affection and love of parents. Nobody taught him the importance of human relation and the feeling. Now, his attitude towards human relation and emotions is just wastage of time. His number one priority is money, power and position. Actually our new generation is gradually developing in such mindset, and we the parents are also responsible for such development.

I used to see how a young son tortures his parents to grab his parents 'lifelong earned money. He is only concerned how to acquire the huge portion of their money. Obviously this act is not acceptable in any way. But a question arises there. Should the son only be held responsible for such behaviour? Such mindset to grab the money clearly indicates the lower moral values of the son. But, is this not the failure in the part of his parent who failed to give his children right moral values? Of course, there is a failure in the part of his parent who couldn't develop such value in his children to pay such respect and care to his parent. In many cases, parents are completely negligent towards their children. Because of this negligent behaviour of parents, they lose their respect and care from their children.

It is just a very simple fact, that is, "what we give that returns back to us in many ways"

BOOKS AND ASSOCIATION

The new generation is so focused towards courses books. They have no time to even think and see beyond the syllabus book. Syllabus books are closely related to their examination and career. Books and our friends have great impact in our life and it's applicable to both good and bad things, which we learn and implement in our life. Great books and friends create great impact.

Our new generation are very helpless; unfortunately all the sources don't give right moral values to our young generation that is why many people get involved in the activities which are not good for our country and for them.

6.03 VISUALIZATION, ACTION AND FEELING

"What you usually think and feel all day long that you become—Emerson"

In our daily life, we meet many people, some of them have great desire to be a big business man, and some has a strong desire to be a big leader. But just a few could be able to achieve their coveted goal. One thing I practically noticed is once they have started to act like a successful businessman, they have started to act like a successful leader. Many of them have started to practice the great law of mind. Our visualization and action becomes a very powerful tool to attract our coveted position.

I had a great passion to drive car and all types of vehicle. At childhood I made a wooden toy vehicle with ball bearings and attached a steering wheel to the front wheels by which I was controlling its movement exactly in my desired direction. It had no engine, so my sister was pushing on the floor and I was just realizing that actually I am driving a car. I was turning the toy car just like today I use to drive my car very sharply and feeling that I am driving a car truly. Mentally I was feeling about actual driving. At childhood stage I was not playing this game intentionally, I was just enjoying the feeling of driving a car. But this mental feeling made me capable to purchase my first car at the age of thirty years old. Although my family back ground was not so favourable for the vehicle. The point I want to describe is that our visualization and strong feeling provide the desired things. Even now I always enjoy long driving; it is just a fun for me. I can say that driving is my passion.

Whatever you want to be in your life you must be passionate about that. Your passion will keep on searching those things which will help you to visualize and feel that you have already achieved. You have to involve your subconscious mind; and it will be in search round the clock to fulfil your desired things.

Go to any forest and see the variety of creatures and living things. All the creatures have the capability to change its body and behaviour which is suitable to keep them alive in their environments. Every day they have to patrol a long distance for the fulfilment of food requirements. Every creature changes its body very interestingly best suitable for hunting and to hide it from other big creatures which can eat it. For example, lizards develop a very specific capability to change the colour of its body. It helps to catch insects and prevents from other reptiles who can hunt him. My point is how it has the capability to do so. How has it enlarged its tongue many times long in comparison to its body? The reason is very simple which gives us a great fact to change our body and mind. The lizard has no God gifted speciality in him, but it has a power of feeling and visualization. It just feels what colour is required for hiding and the colour of its body changes accordingly. Its tongue gets enlarged many times to its body length just due to strong desire and feeling.

Human is a great intellectual, and he had mostly focused only to the power of thinking, but just few are realizing the power of feelings. The most dangerous thing is that due to ignorance, we use our power of feeling which is going against our own. It is very sad that we do not get the benefit of the power of feeling while we are using due to ignorance just against our life. How it works? To understand this fact, we can realize how our body reacts with the nightmare.

Everyone has an experience of nightmare. What happens when we dream a nightmare? We get frightened badly, and our body shows all the symptoms as if we are actually in some danger. Sweating starts, our breathing becomes rigorous as it happens at the time of danger. Many times we sough and even start to cry. The fact is whatever we feel that actually happens to our body too. It does not matter just after awaking we become normal. The truthiness of the event is not so important, but the important thing is the strong feeling. When our mind has no doubt then the feeling immediately reflects in our body.

If you are unhappy due to any reason, how we change our mood. There is a very simple method, just start acting as a very happy man. Initially, it appears very funny but gradually our inner mind will accept it and our body will behave accordingly. The basic is to convey any feeling to our subconscious.

A man went to a laboratory and gave his blood sample for some allergic test. By mistake, he received the cancer report of some other patient. The very normal person when he read the report and knew that cancer has been detected in his body, he was shocked. All of sudden he started to feel very weak, and a strong belief developed in his mind that he will not survive for more days. He didn't clarify about the genuineness of the report. Actually he never thought the report may be wrong. His health started to deteriorate day by day and he was admitted to a hospital and after many checks, doctor was surprised to see there was no disease which may deteriorate his health so speedily. Later it revealed that the report was actually of some other person who was suffering from cancer disease. Then the doctor explained how the wrong report of some other person was mistakenly given his name. After he started to feel gradually a bit normal, it took a week for him to become completely normal.

This is a very practical example which shows how our adverse feel due to any false reason affects our body as if it is absolutely true. So, the actual event is a fact but what we feel about the event creates great effect to our mind and body.

Our feeling changes our body and mind accordingly. Our thinking creates our feeling and our mood. When we think about happy moment in our life a feeling of happiness develops in our mind, while thinking about unpleasant moment creates an unpleasant feeling in our mind. Most of the successful people always have a smiling face. The smiling facial expression is not just a matter of showing but actually always habitual to maintain their happy mood. Their happy feeling plays a great role in attracting happy things and happy moments in their life. We used to see people who show generally unpleasant mood, this increases the opportunity of actually unpleasant situation.

We must be aware about our thinking and feeling. We can list down ten and more things which can play as mood changer elements. Whenever we feel bad immediately we can change our feeling.

6.04 DREAM, DESIRE AND ACTION MUST BE ALIGNED

Now a day a joke is very popular about Santa. He started his prayer to God to have a son. He worshiped in most of the famous temples and travelled almost big temples all over India. His prayer was very rigorous and was praying all the way for the fulfilment of his desire for a son. His worship was so hard and intense. God became afraid and appeared in front of Santa and said, everything is OK but "my lord first you get married."

This is a very interesting story which describes that many people put their huge efforts for achieving any particular goal but they miss the most basic things which is first required.

Let us suppose that I am living in Kanpur and I want to go to New Delhi by my car. I pray to God too much to reach New Delhi but unknowingly I am driving my car on Grand Trunk Road in the direction of Kolkata. Is it possible for me to reach New Delhi? Of course not, despite our regular and honest prayer; I can blame God that the prayer doesn't work. In the second case, I am driving my car in the right direction towards New Delhi and not praying to God. I may be surprised to see that I have reached the destination without praying to God.

The conclusion of this very simple example is very big and explains all the reason of success and failure. If we are doing very hard work in the wrong direction, then despite all prayers we will not be able to reach our destination. Most people condemn that they are very unfortunate since despite their hard work and very big worship to God they couldn't succeed in their life in a particular mission. They don't understand how to make their effort in the right direction. The problem is not they are unfortunate but they are not able to understand that their direction of action is wrong.

The work done in wrong direction

What hard work we do?

How much hard work we do?

How much time we do hard?

All these will not make us reach our goal if the direction is wrong. But any small effort which is done in the right direction will make us advance to our destination. The fact is we don't know how we are making several mistakes in the wrong direction and condemning our God or our destiny. It is a general experience in offices where a very few people have no adequate knowledge to work on a computer. All of this is just due to their indifferent approach towards the computer. They feel many difficulties in working on a computer and they feel problems due to their lack of knowledge, their response wills be like a pre-recorded cassette as "system is not working." The fact is the person does not know how to work but his way of statement represents that he is efficient but due to the problem in computer system he couldn't do his work. This is the basic approach which represents the way of behaviour of general people. Since computer does not oppose his statement in any ways, he puts the blame on the system.

By this way people put their failure and inefficiency to God and his destiny. Their way of expression is such as they are doing all the things in the right way but God or their luck is not favouring them. It is very easy to convince other people since majority of people believes that almighty God has created this world, and we all are just like a puppet in the hand of God. This belief is nothing but a very popular and widely accepted excuse for our inefficiency and our failure. God never bother to make someone failed or to make someone successful.

We ride cycle and practice the skill to keep balanced against the gravitational force. We also learned how they have to ride cycle at the turning according to the surface of the road. Whenever we cross the limit accident happens. We can't blame the gravitational force and frictional force. Gravitation and friction are just forces it doesn't try to protect anyone or try to make anyone fall. These forces help people to move forward if they move in right alignment. If they violate the forces, they will fall down and accident happens.

We have to learn and practice the skill to align with these forces and we will get great help from these forces. So, bear in mind very clearly that God doesn't make anyone lucky and someone unlucky. These are just a perception developed due to escaping tendency of human.

6.05 FROM OUR TRADITIONAL WORK TO OUR DREAM PROJECT

This is really a great problem to make the four factors in one direction. But it is also a fact that there is a solution for every problem. We can divide our life stages into two parts.

1. Up to an age of twenty years, we are free to choose our profession according to our passion. Up to this stage, we have all the options opened, and we can choose one which is mostly suitable to our passion and reason. This is an ideal time and opportunity to choose any particular profession as per our inner desire which is best suitable to fulfil our passion. Although this is the best suitable time for choosing the goal, it is not possible for people who have such awareness in the importance of identifying their passion and to decide a particular field. But most of the people are not so aware at this. When the awareness comes in mind, they will be in some other field and in many cases the field in which they are working may not be their dream work and it is not so easy to change their profession at that stage of their career.
2. This is the stage in which any person is absorbed but this field is not fulfilling his passion. The problem is he can't change his job at this stage. Then what is the option? Is it the dead end of his dream work? Of course not, although the options are limited, options are available even at these stages. It's OK but it is not so easy to change the track instantly. At this stage, first, we have to identify our passion very carefully, and then list down the possible field that can be done during our free time from our regular job or business work. It can be divided as 10:00 AM to 5:00 PM for our regular job which is essential for meeting our financial and social requirements. And 5:00 PM to 10:00 PM can be utilized for the work which is really our dream project. This method will be very safe for shifting towards our dream project. At initial stage our traditional work will be primary and our dream project will be secondary.

And, after the growth of our secondary project, we can migrate ourselves completely to our dream project.

Suppose I am working in any ABC company which is my primary job. And I start a secondary job which is really my passion. I can start this dream project when I get free time from my regular job in the ABC Company. The secondary work is not chosen for money, but it will satisfy my pleasure. This is a work which really gives me job satisfaction and pleasure. Later on, the secondary work which has been started for pleasure may grow so big that the free time may not be enough to continue. When the financial earning increases sufficiently enough to meet our all requirements, we can decide to migrate completely to our dream work.

Your dream, desire and action mentally and physically must be aligned and in one direction.

It is a very big misconception "Only intelligent and talented man becomes successful." Of course intelligence is a vital factor which plays a big role in success. What are the key factors which make a man successful? Many researches happened and life history has been studied. If we list down all the conclusions derived by different studies then it may cross more than hundred points. Summarizing these points, few points will come out.

- Know your passion
- Strong reason
- Clear vision
- Consistent action
- Firm determination

I found several factors which contribute a lot in success, which are basically based on these four basic points.

KNOW YOUR PASSION

Narayan Kartiken says in a TV advertisement that "Driving is my passion." This is a very important dialogue which represents the importance of passion.

In a volleyball game the height is a very important factor for a best volleyball player. But it is not the only factor which makes a player best.

I used to see the volleyball game which is being played every day in front of my balcony. One day I saw they were adjusting the height of the net. Suddenly I realized that internationally the height is fixed in such a way that everybody should not reach it easily. But it should not be so high that nobody could reach.

It is a very important point to note.

Height should not be too low so that everyone can do smash hit.

Height should not be too high so that nobody can do smash hit.

In the first case if it is too low then, it will not be challenging and the charm and enthusiasm will be lost since anybody will be able to do smash hit. Both the great player and average player will appear just the same since even an average player will be able to smash hit and score. Actually height like an eight feet is a challenging height which works as a filter to segregate the winners from the average players.

A perfect smash hit depends on many factors like

- Right jump
- Right hit
- Right placing

These three factors combine and make a perfect hit which fetches point. Player who practices daily actually practices this skill for right hit for earning points. It requires persistent practice and high motivation level.

The height of the net will work as a filter. Similarly everybody wants to escape from challenges in their life. But this is the challenge which segregates the winners from the collection of mass people. This is the challenge which motivates us to enhance our skill, strategy and strength.

There are different categories of people who have some different goal from this game. Just a few has a goal to make this goal as their career and they dream to go to state level and national level game. Their dressing and their commitment and involvement level are very high. They learn the technique and practice the technique on a regular basis. They develop their proficiency in skill to earn points. They are filled with great commitment for their practice and enhance their performance on a regular basis. They are the player of category 1. The second category of people is those who have great interest and motivation for the game but couldn't achieve their desired level. They play the game for pleasure and for their past attachment to the game. There are also a third category people who have no future goal in this game, but used to play this game for their health requirement and meeting people.

These three categories of people are found in any organization. Category one people who are very ambitious. They perform greatly. They rise in their career speedily. Their commitment level is very high for organizational growth. This category of people really gives direction and leads the organization. These people are assets of the organization.

Category two—people who were very ambitious in the past and now their level has come down. They work for the organization. Their comment level is fairly high for organizational growth. This category also plays a great role in the business growth of the organizations.

Category three—these people work in a very causal manner and their commitment level is very low to the organizations. They work just as they are passing their time in the organization. These people are just a liability to the organizations.

6.06 PERCEPTION

How our perception works? There was a baby elephant which was tied with a strong chain. He was trying his level best to break the chain and to make him free, but all efforts failed. Gradually, he perceived that he can never be able to break the chain and make himself free. His subconscious mind conceived the fact about his inability to break the chain. The baby elephant perceived in his mind that he can't break the chain. The baby elephant grows as a young giant elephant. Now it is quite easy to break the chain in a moment. Now, the elephant was tied by an ordinary rope which is very easy to break. Moreover, the young and strong elephant never tries to break the rope. His perception which has been formed in his mind at his early stage prevents him to make effort to break since he feels that he cannot break according to his perception. He never makes any effort to break it only due to his earlier perception about his incapability.

"Our perceptions make us capable or incapable to do anything."

Perception is just a combination of real event and our own thinking which results in conclusion. Perception is just our conclusion based on our past experiences. Sometime it is correct and many times it is wrong. Our perception about us plays a crucial role in our development. Our wrong perception hampers our development. It is just a false brief. Many a times our wrong perception until rectified, much of our valuable time is lost. For example most of the poor people live with a perception that they are very unfortunate and they will remain poor forever. This is just a wrong perception which keeps them poor lifelong.

Here are some examples of wrong perception:

1. I am an unlucky person
2. My memory is very poor
3. Only smart and talented people can be successful
4. I couldn't get opportunity for success
5. I have no family support for great performance

Our perceptions may be right or wrong. But according to its nature, positive or negative, both cases affect our life in positive and negative way.

These negative perceptions spoil our whole life. Many people never overcome their negative beliefs. If our perception is wrong then it is very difficult to be successful in any field of our life.

Perception and attitude can be changed but in a gradual manner. It is quite difficult and almost impossible to change our attitude and perception overnight. However in some cases perception may change overnight but not attitude.

I heard the Indian Prime Minister Shri Narendra Modi addressing the children. He described his way of thinking and working. In this context he gave a great message. He said,

"Never dream to be something in life but dream to do something in life"

He gave a very important message of life to the children, which is based on the basic need of pleasure in life. His message was very important since it encouraged the development of an attitude to enjoy your work. When we enjoy our work then everything happens great without any tension. This attitude yields great perfection and improves our productivity. When we do not enjoy our work then it is done half-heartedly and lot of problems arise due to imperfect work.

WE HAVE TO PAY THE COST OF INCOMPLETE INFORMATION

WE HAVE TO PAY THE COST OF INCOMPLETE WORK.

We can divide the people broadly into two categories according to their habitual thinking.

- I can do it — Solution mode
- I can't do it — Problem mode

One person says "I can do it." Another person says "I cannot do it." These two statements reflect our thinking pattern and how it affects our pattern of thinking.

The first person says that I can do it then he switches on his mind to find out how it can be done. His mind is activated to find out the solution. Whatever we say our whole mind finds out all the possible facts to prove the statement right. In this way mind do many mental exercise to find out the probable solution. This type of personality keeps a person's mind in solution mode. To be in solution mode become his natural thinking process. Basic statement of this type of people is "It is difficult but can be done." This is the best example of positive people, who finds a solution on every situation. They smile in every situation and are always thankful to everyone. In this pattern our mind keeps on thinking the possible solution round the clock. So the conclusion is we put our mind either in solution mode or in problem mode.

Solution mode sees solution in every problem.

Problem mode sees problem in every solution.

To be in solution mode or in problem mode doesn't depend on the situation but it is just a matter of our habitual thinking.

Now we discuss the second category people. They always think and talk what they cannot do. This pattern of thinking switches his mind against finding the possible solution. This statement switches off his mind since he thinks he cannot do. Then there is no question to put any effort for finding the possible solution. The activity of his mind stopped due to his feeling about his inability to do that. He basic thinking is "It may be possible but very difficult." His pattern of usual thinking makes him fearful and makes him annoyed to everybody.

As per the law of our mind, our mind and body behaves according to our habitual thinking and our belief.

6.07 HIGHLIGHTS OF THIS CHAPTER

1. The basic difference between human and animal is the capability of dreaming. If we are not dreaming and we are not doing something for a big dream, then we must think as a human what we are doing?

2. By birth what am I was not in our hand, but what should be in our life up to death is of course is in my hand. I am the creator of my destiny.
3. Successful and failed all uses certain fixed sets of vocabulary often, which represent their core belief about success and failure. These core beliefs mould their destiny and life accordingly. These statements strengthen their belief strongly to its nature.
4. Visualization and realization of future goal are very powerful tools to attract in our life. Unknowingly we use these powerful tools against our life due to ignorance and habitually negative thinking and attitudes.
5. Our dream, desire, action and belief must be in one direction only then we attain our goal, otherwise our lots of efforts will nullify each other, and despite a lot of efforts we will not be able to achieve our goal in our life.
6. Switching over from our traditional job to our dream project is also a matter of strong belief. It is also a matter of testing how strong is our dream and what is the level of our inner confidence to our dream project? The work on our dream project between 5:00 PM to 10:00 PM is the ideal way to gradual switching over to our dream project.
7. Our perception and our conception play a vital role in determining our life and our destiny. Our determination becomes our destiny, if it is strong enough. Nature doesn't care whether our perception is right or wrong. It just provides to our life according to the nature of our perceptions.

7. Moral Values

7.01 POWER MINUS MORAL VALUES

- Those who want to do something for country have no power.
- Those who have power have no actual interest to serve for the country.
- Those who have power and desire to do for our country; they are helpless in democratic systems.

Very high qualification and professional skill gives very high capacity to earn money. He gets a powerful position which gives money, power and position. He becomes capable to buy all the luxuries and comforts. However, if he has no moral values in life then his power and position lead him towards illegal activities and even crime since his greed for power and money increases day by day.

Powerful position with high moral value brings peace and happiness in life and it becomes a great asset for his family, society and for country. It always works for the welfare of poor and needy person of the society. Power in high-valued person is a boon for the society. Just like an atomic energy, it is a great power which is used for the welfare of humanity. However, if the nuclear power goes to the extremist, it will be used for destruction of humanity. Similarly, power itself is not good or bad, it depends on the person who has the power. Positive person always use the power for constructive work whereas negative person will use power and position always in a bad manner.

POWER + WISDOM	=	HAPPY AND SATISFIED LIFE
	=	ASSETS FOR SOCIETY/COUNTRY
POWER – WISDOM	=	UNHAPPY AND UNSATISFIED LIFE
	=	LIABILITY FOR SOCIETY/COUNTRY

Everybody realize that crime and scams are increasing day by day. It is really a matter of concern since the speed will increase in compounding way as the time will go further.

Those who are very brilliant, they mostly focus on their examination and they perform excellent in competitive exams. They almost neglect the part of value education; actually they feel that these are just meaningless things. Great desire for power and position makes them focused to examination, the mostly qualified for higher and powerful position in the society. They get most of the valuable post in government department. Since they have no moral, their work style creates a lot of corruptions in the society. But those who have good moral values mostly legged behind the corrupt people and the highly valued person couldn't be able to reach higher post in comparison to the corrupt people. This is the main reason why corruption increases day by day. Our judicial system couldn't panelise a politician who does scam due to legal complication, since the corrupt position uses the loopholes of our judiciary systems. He motivates thousands of young people to do scam. A belief develops in the mind of people that you can escape even after a crime if you have contacts and money and other powers. The respect to our judiciary system is lost in the mind of general people.

In such situation, the confidence and pride of criminals increase and the confidence and pride of law binding and disciplined people decrease. These situations are very dangerous and harmful for any state of a country.

Everybody blames that law is not doing its work properly. But the fact is law itself is not a living thing. It is just handled by the person whose intention is not right. When crime-oriented person handles the law then he will find the loopholes for the protection of criminals. Big lawyers are so learned they can prove an innocent person as a criminal, and they can prove a criminal as an innocent person. It is very frustrating that the knowledge and deep study of lawyers are used for the protection of criminals.

In any society if the moral of the creative and real high-valued people is low, then this society will never develop. The fact is creative and constructive people play a pioneer role in the development of society. But if these people live in insecure feeling, they will not be able to contribute their idea and thoughts which will develop the society.

Those people should be provided comfort and luxuries, only then they will give their contribution in social around development. But in many countries, the criminal and destructive people are provided protection and luxuries. But ultimately society will have to pay the cost. Provision of security and luxuries to destructive people always develops crime and destruction in society.

Constructive and creative people always work for the upliftment of the society. Whichever country has neglected the creative and great scholars had to pay the cost of negligence. Many great scholars migrate to another country. Then they get benefited with the innovation of scholars.

United States is treated as a most advanced country in the world. It has provided such a suitable and comfortable environment for genius; it attracts talents from all over the world. It is very interesting that a student born and brought up in any country choose to work in the United States. Of course, their provision and arrangement for the talented people are marvellous and extremely suitable to them.

When any talents are appreciated and recognized, it grows rapidly and works for constructive and development work for the country. High appreciation and recognition of talent are the basic reason for the growth of talent and attraction for a new talent. If any country fails to provide such things then the event of brain drain happens. And then talents are used for the purpose of money earning.

✦ *It is the responsibility of the country to provide appreciation and recognition to all the talented people who are working on any creative work for the country, otherwise the talented will start working for earning money only and the talent will not work for creative work.*

Many countries are facing acute problem of brain drain.Those who couldn't go to other country start to use their talent as a tool for earning money, name and fame. Their creative talents are not being used for research work, or creative work in any field which may play a great role in the development of the country.

If the government don't provide recognition and luxuries to researchers and scholars who are engaged in research work and great creative work then they start to use their creative talent in earning money, name and fame. It becomes a big loss to the country. This is the main reason why Nobel Prize winners mostly come from the developed country.

Country should take care of such especially talented people. These people if given proper care will contribute greatly to country. And an environment will develop where many talented people will be involved in creative works for the country.

I ask young aspirants who are about to pass out from technical institutions and from college, "what is your future plan?" Everybody says for better and secure job which should have handsome salary package. In our country, handsome salary package, power and position are the area of focus. Any student is treated as successful if he has achieved any of these things. But money is the prime focus of their life.

It is a matter of concern that nobody choose to go for research work in any field, nobody aims to do some creative work in any field like literature, like economics and other subjects. This mindset of our younger generation is really a matter of concern. But the question is who is responsible for this? It is the collective responsibility of government and policy makers. They couldn't be able to create such an environment in which general people could see the lucrative position of scientist and researchers, and all the people who are working in the field for creative contribution towards country. I don't say country is not doing anything in this area; my feeling is it should do more, so that a mass appeal must develop to our younger generation.

Three areas play a vital role in nation building, which prepares generation for nation building. If they don't do their role in proper way then generation spoils. And development of the nation will be affected badly.

✦ Education Systems	Teachers and educational institutions.
✦ Law making bodies	Politicians
✦ Law implementing bodies	Judiciary system and police

These three categories play a vital role in positive development of generation which gives right direction to the development of the country. However every one of our citizen knows very well the real qualities of the people who are working in this field.

It is a well-known fact that crimes and illegal activities are not increasing due to the activities of bad people, but it is due to the inactiveness of the good people. Dominance of people having bad track record and crime minded people has increased at a large scale. So the constructive and high-valued people are disappearing gradually. So, these areas have been totally handled by people who do not a vision for the growth of country. They have their prime focus to earn huge money by name, fame and by power. They have one point agenda about earning huge money by their power and position.

It is a matter of great concern that our education system has prime focus to make a student capable to get handsome salary package. The quality of the person doesn't matter for them. All the big educational institutions are run by corporate, for whom institutions are just like a factory which prepares doctors, engineers and other professional who are capable to earn huge money.

A great line I found:

Nation First, Institution Second, Individual Last.

I felt it is a great line, but in fact, practically, most of the person feels in just the reverse order. They feel individual first and then institution, country they don't bother about.

7.02 QUALITY OF PEOPLE DETERMINATION

Many people believe that power corrupts a man. But I don't believe this perception. I think something in a different way. It is a fact that when a person reaches to some powerful position he starts to do something wrong due to his power and position. We conclude that power made him corrupt.

Money and power doesn't make a man corrupt but it expands and demonstrates the actual quality of people. Every person is very polite and courteous in behaviour with higher officers or any powerful person, but the quality is tested on his behaviour with those people who are very weak in power and position in comparison to him. If his behaviour towards weak person is good, then the quality is really good. When we are in weak position then our real character doesn't appear for the external people. However as we get some power and position then our actual quality comes out and real face gets displayed to other people. If I possess inherited desire of corruption, then it will come out immediately when I get some position.

Real kind hearted people will help more people when they are in a good position. Other corrupt people will start to exploit the weaker person when they get some power.

Immature people when gets power, he thinks to rule over all the people. He feels very anxious to display, and makes several efforts to display his position that he is very powerful. His abnormal behaviour to display his powerful position makes many stupid mistakes for which he have to pay.

India's population is very high. That's why a huge number of people are unemployed. Due to this high density of population, the number of unemployed youth and unemployed person is very high. This high unemployment provides very cheaper labour and workers. To hire a person at home is very cheaper and very average people use house helper and maid servant. The low quality people exploit their servant and maid servant inhumanly. The saddest thing is the behaviour; they don't behave with them like a human being. The way a man treats a person who is working for him and being paid for his work is very poor. The way they treat such weaker people reflects the quality of them.

As an employer, he has the right to take work from him since he is paying for that. But, he must always treat such people as a human being since they are also human. I have seen a few people who are fond of their pet. They pay too much love and affection and timely care towards a pet but they never treat a fraction of respect towards human being in comparison to their pet. This attitude towards a human being reflects the level of our humanity and moral values.

A person may be poor and he may work for me in my home or in my concern but his feeling, as a human being, must be respected. If one fails to do that, then it is a deficiency in the part of his personality.

It is a law of nature that in rainy season river overflows, whereas the huge sea shows no or any effect on its pattern of behaviour in any season. It is also observed that non-deserving people have great desire for their respect, but real deserving people don't bother for all of these things.

7.03 SKILL OF PRODUCTION AND MARKETING

It can be illustrated by an example of production and marketing of any product. Let us take an example of a soap production. It is broadly classified into two categories.

- Production of soap
- Marketing of soap

These two segments complete the business of soap manufacturing unit. A successful business unit requires the quality of the soap to be the best. Production of soap is one part which requires setting up a production unit and hiring skilled labours. All of this section requires capital, and those who have capital they can start a soap manufacturing unit. It also requires many skills apart from the capital. But real skill requirement is marketing promotion and marketing of the products where we have to compete with big players who are already established in the market.

Here it is very difficult to establish a new brand in the competitive market. A lot of factors are required in establishing a product in the market:

1. Quality of the products
2. Pricing of the products
3. Promotion of the products
4. Some innovation in the products

7.04 HYPOCRISY OF LIFE

"Simplicity is the best style but only the great mind can afford it."

unknown

Life started from ancient time since then hypocrisy is an integral part of life. But as the human society developed and its power of thinking developed, this hypocrisy developed many times in human life. But the important question is why hypocrisy becomes an integral part of our human life and behaviour?

As we know that "Pleasure Instinct" is a very important factor which drives our activity and our life. For this pleasure instinct another desire develops that is desire to prove "I am the best." Desire to prove that I am the best is the root factor of hypocrisy in human life.

Everybody has some inherited tendency which they got by birth. Later he acquires many other tendencies from his parent and environment where he grows. All of these prepare his particular way of thinking and behaviour. But in the society where he lives and deals, some different behaviour which is acceptable by a so-called civilized society is required. Our actual way of thinking and the way of behaviours are not acceptable. Then we start to behave like the one which is acceptable. This is the way how hypocrisy starts in our life. For example we are not honest but we project ourselves as honest. We are not generous but we behave as we are very generous. We behave in a different way like something than what we actually are.

As our society and human intelligence have developed, complexity and hypocrisy have increased. As complexity and hypocrisy increases, we lose the beauty of life. Have you ever noticed that children of any country look very cute and lovely? Child of any animal looks very lovely. The reason behind their beauty is their innocence. There is no contradiction in their inner and external behaviour. Their honesty and innocence makes them lovely.

I know a very famous beautician of India. Whenever I see her I don't feel any beauty. I feel that any child if sees her, he may be frightened by looking her face. Over makeup virtually makes her virtually ugly and very furious. If I try to make my speech very much impressive then the beauty of my speech will get lost. If I try to project myself very much honest then it indicates that I am not an honest man.

It is very interesting how politicians make a huge noise, and project him the friendliest person to the public. All of them claim that to politics just to chatter his desire to serve the nation.

I always believe that simple style is the most beautiful style.

A poor man wants to project himself as a rich man.

A dishonest man wants to project himself as an honest man.

7.05 HIGHLIGHTS OF THIS CHAPTER

1. The most painful thing in our country is to have people who have no moral values in a powerful position.
2. Our law making body, law implementing body and responsibility for creation of high-valued people are in the hands of those people whose moral values are very low. Most corruption is involved in politician, judiciary, police and education systems.
3. Power with no moral values develops corruption in personal and social life.

4. Power plus wisdom makes a happy life and assets for the country. Power minus wisdom makes an unhappy life and becomes a liability to the country.
5. If any person commits criminal offence and not penalized within a certain time frame, it motivates thousands of young generation to commit criminal offence. And the high moral people suffer from fear in such society.

8. Expand Your Orbit

8.01 STORY OF HUMAN ORIGINATION FROM MONKEY

Human is treated as the most developed and sophisticated animal of this world. It is very interesting to know how human has been developed so much while other creatures were not able to make themselves so much advanced as human. Darwin and Lamark gave the concept of "Survival of fittest." This theory explains very clearly that those who had changed mentally and physically according to the environment could have survived and others were eliminated by the environment. Everyone knows that most of the creatures decreased and many were eliminated while the number of human was increasing very fast.

Many facts proved that man has been developed from monkey. Just a very small group of monkeys started to walk on its two feet. They thought that while they can walk on their two feet, then why their four feet should be involved. Soon they realized the benefit of walking by two feet. They started to see their enemies and hunt from distance which made their life easy and their chances of survival better. Two feet became free and had been used as hands and it holds arms which increased their attacking capacity and also their defence. These changes made them completely different from the other monkeys. These monkeys later developed as human. The concept is how a very small change becomes so bigger in a long run. Now human feel hesitated to accept that monkeys are their ancestors. So a wide difference has developed and human has become so much advanced in comparison to monkey.

I saw that many person started a particular job and continued to the same job life long, while a few started his profession as a labour and he expanded his orbit day by day and reached to the top of the profession. What are the basic difference in their pattern of thinking and their belief? I found that was some basic differences in their pattern of thinking. The differences in their mindset lead them to the different levels in their life.

1. Risk-bearing capacity
2. They don't accept their present job for life long
3. They have the ability to take responsibility
4. They have confidence in their ability
5. Ability to face the challenges
6. Daring to do something new

Physically every person is looking same but their dream and vision are different in size and shape which makes them different from other.

What is a dream? Some replied that dream is picture in a sequence which we see during sleep. Then the great personality modified the definition as "Dream is not a picture in sequence which we see during sleep, but the real dream is that which don't make us sleep." Really it is an anxiety to do something bigger, something great. A person may lose his wealth, he may lose his health but the biggest sad thing is when he loses his dream in his life to do something bigger, something great in his life. Dream is the basic thing which makes us different from animal and also makes us different from other even human being also. Just imagine if Wright brothers had not dreamed to fly in the sky. Just think Charles Babbage had not invented the computing device which is developed as modern computers.

The person who has great dream and vision has changed the world. They had dared to dream big. They had dreamed to do something different in the world. Their madness to find something new has always given something unique which had changed the life style of the whole world. They have changed the perception of human.

8.02 HOW BRITISH RULED ALL OVER INDIA

British came to India in 1600 AD. The purpose was trading with India. It made it's headquarter at Calcutta. During the process of business, it studied the Indian social culture and the conflict among the thousands of small and big states.

As the business expanded British Government establishment gaining power and started to acquire the weak states by providing them all the means. It may be it is in form of support by fund and by the help of army support. Gradually it gained power and started to acquire other states applying different means. In many cases it applied the principle of divide and rule. The strange thing is it has not done anything in all of a sudden. But, it applied its expansion policy gradually. And the time came it has expanded its regime all over the country. Very interesting learning is given by the whole tenure of British rule. British ruled almost three and half century over India.

It has acquired the states one by one strategy. It has never tried to overcome the country in one instance. So, achievement part by part has been adopted for expansion of British rule. When you acquire any territory then your confidence, capability and skill grows up which helps and makes easy the next assignment. It has started with those states which were comparatively week and easy to acquire.

The conclusion of the British rule can be summarized as follows.

- Starts with easy target
- Completion of easy target gives confidence and capability for next bigger assignments
- Expand your orbit daily
- You become more powerful if your strategy and technology are more advanced than your stronger opponent

8.03 STRATEGY AND TECHNOLOGY ARE THE MOST DECIDING FACTORS

Now we are living in information age. Information and technology have changed every sphere of human life and human society. In ancient time when it was a stone age the fights between people happened by the use of stones and nails. Now we have prepared knifes, swords, sophisticated guns and even missiles. All of the weapons are the expansion of stones and nails to make the fight more dangerous. We have expanded the effectiveness of stones and nail by the use of advanced technologies and researches. Wars and battles were mostly dependent on the number of our manpower. By the development of technology now the wars are mostly dependent on advanced technology. Number of man power is not a deciding factor in comparison to technology.

Of course we are Indian and it is very painful to accept that British Government had ruled nearly three and half century over India. We have to accept these facts that strategically and technologically they were more advanced than us and that is why they became capable to rule our country over such a long period.

A very famous saying is "Attack is the best way of defence." The history of our India reveals that a large number of foreign intruders kept on attacking India. It is very strange to see that a large number of attacks happened on India whereas India has not attacked any other country in history. And whatever it has attacked is basically retaliation against other attackers.

It is very important to understand that why such a large attack happened to our country. The reason is behind our defensive mindset and culture. From ancient time India was treated as pioneer of religious activities. People used to come to India for learning religious things and practices. So the mass people were guided by the principles and laws of religions. Attacking other countries were against the law of mass culture, people who were living were contented and the values received from religion had great impact in their mindset and lifestyle.

This entire factor made them very defensive. This message of peaceful people spread all over the world and attracted them to attack over our country. They have looted and murdered brutally millions of Indian people. Our history is witness.

In this chain Hoons, Sak, Sinkader the great Mughals and British all had come here and damaged our country very badly. Till now we see and hear that extremist are being trained and they are send to our country to operate massive killing and destruction in India. But even now we don't involve in such activity to intrude for destruction in neighbouring country.

8.04 PICKUP A PARTICULAR THING AND DEVELOP MASTERY WILL BE THE SOLUTION OF EVERYTHING

Remember the ustad Bismillah Khan who had got Bharat Ratna for his excellent performance and contribution in Shahnai playing. It is very interesting to note that how he devoted his whole life to a very ordinary musical instrument Shahnai. He whole-heartedly involved in playing his musical instrument lifelong. He added many dimensions to this instrument which never has been observed. It is very important how his involvement to such an instrument gave him so much reputation not in India but all around the world. It is a marvellous example which shows how our mastery and perfection in a particular area give everything, and many things which are beyond our imagination. If our activity related to a particular thing expands day by day, then it attracts everything in our life in terms of name, fame, satisfaction, power and positions everything.

Think about Sachin Tendulkar a great cricket player who has no expertise in any other field except cricket. Only cricket is his passion, cricket is his love and cricket is his life. This so intense focus made him the God of cricket. Such focus made him an outstanding performer and this cricket gave him everything which general people can't even imagine in their life.

What happens when we take works in multiple areas and when we do in any particular area? Our activity in multiple areas divides our focus, energy and time. Division in focus and energy decreases our performance. When we pay undivided our focus energy and time to a particular activity the quality and quantity goes high very much. Suppose, Tendulkar would practice cricket, Lawn Tennis and Table Tennis then could he achieve the level what he has achieved the level in cricket, of course not. And nobody would know him as great cricket star. Full involvement of our mind and body take the game to a different level, which nobody can achieve by divided focus.

Let us think what happens when one particular activity keeps going on in our mind. It gradually expands to all parts of our mind like conscious mind and subconscious mind. When the activity enters in our subconscious mind then it performs its duty round the clock. It is just like a chain reaction and full involvement always provides many new ideas and thought to improve the level of performance. Undivided attention and efforts becomes very effective.

It is also very difficult to work with so much undivided attention and efforts. It is very difficult for those who have no strong reason in their life. Strong reason and clear vision make us focused. Without having any strong reason and clear vision life drift in just like a leaf in air. It is just like a floating log in water which keeps on flowing with the current. It has no clear destination. When a boat is prepared with the log then it has a certain fixed destination towards which it moves.

8.05 GO TO EXTRA MILE

"Raise your bar daily."

This is a mission statement of a high jumper. For an athlete, "go to extra mile daily." Empowered people give it their all, even on their worst days. They're always pushing themselves to go the extra mile. One of Bruce Lee's pupils ran three miles every day with him. One day, they were about to hit the three-mile mark when Bruce said, "Let's do two more." His pupil was tired and said, "I'll die if I run two more." Bruce's response? "Then do it." His pupil became so angry that he finished the full five miles. Exhausted and furious, he confronted Bruce about his comment, and Bruce explained it this way: "Quit and you might as well be dead". If you always put limits on what you can do, physical or anything else, it'll spread over into the rest of your life. It'll spread into your work, into your morality, into your entire being. There are no limits. There are plateaus, but you must not stay there; you must go beyond them.

If it kills you, it kills you. A man must constantly exceed his level." If you aren't getting a little bit better each day, then you're most likely getting a little worse—and what kind of life is that?

8.06 EXPAND YOUR ORBIT

A king visited Japan and a saint gave him a miracle box to him. He said that this is a miracle box which will change your whole life miraculously if you follow the instruction about this box. The king became very eager to know about the condition which required following for keeping the miraculous power of box. The saint replied this box's miracle power is most effective when it is kept in north and south direction exactly. The king brought this box his home and according to the suggestion of the saint he placed the box exactly in the direction of north and south direction by measuring with compass.

Soon the king realized that tables and bed are not in aligned with the box and looking very bad, so the tables and beds had been arranged accordingly. Then the door and window was not in aligned with the box and the beds, so he had to change his whole building according to keep aligned with. Then the other houses are not looking in alignment with the house of the king. Then all the houses have been constructed to make them alignment with the house of king. Gradually the whole things have been changed to keep them aligned with the miraculous box.

This is a very interesting story which shows when one thing is fixed in our house all the other things will be change accordingly. If we establish one thing in our life then other things will change. Suppose a student decides that he will devote eight hours every day for his studies. If he makes a firm decision and he has a capacity to stick on to his decision then automatically many unwanted things will start to eliminate from his routine. If he does not eliminate the unnecessary things then he will not be able to study eight hours. Then a question will arise, either he stick with his decision or will continue to live as usual. Since any person has limited time twenty-four hours, if his resolution is strong then automatically other unnecessary activities will be eliminated gradually.

If a student decides that he will go to bed at 11:00 PM and get up at 5:00 AM then many activities which are not matching with this schedule will start to eliminate automatically. If a student associated with such a boy whose priority is not study, then this association will disturb his study also.

Our core value is just a pivot point around which our feeling and activity revolves. I found many boys who have a very strong belief that job can't be secured by study only but it is matter of high contact and by paying huge money anyone can get a job. Since his core belief is job can be secured by spending money, he involved in making contact with such people who work in such type of middle man activity. Generally it is observed that many have been trapped with middle man and lost a handsome amount. Many believe that without illegal activity nobody can be a rich man. The most dangerous thing that they start to move on illegal path and most of them trapped such as they can never be able to reverse back.

My simple view is that our core value leads our life on the positive way or negative way. Our core values are nothing but our perception. Which are formed in our life from our childhood?

Recently, I met a very successful businessperson at his home. That fellow regularly travels to many cities for his business concern and deals. His family was very frustrated with him due to his excessive involvement in his profession. He really spent most of his time travelling places and merely had any time for his family. It was due to these frequent trips and exhaustion, his health was deteriorating. I tried to figure out what exactly was the motivating factor that involved him so intensely. The answer I found was that he was enjoying the expansion of his business and rising profits. The pleasure of expansion was so intense that he hardly cared for anything else. Even his family or his health matters less. He focused on expansion of his business alone.

8.07 EXPANSION GIVES PLEASURE

Challenges make a man strong, smart and skilled

A very important aspect of human nature is visible in this story. That is pleasure is directly proportional to expansion. Among all, expansion of achievement is the most important thing that is associated with pleasure. In this case, he is not lacking money. Rather, 'He is trapped in a number game'. His business will be joyful only until it will be expanding. Whenever the expansion stops the interest and charm lost immediately. It will be dull for him. Now money is no big factor for his livelihood but a tool for his mental satisfaction.

Have you ever thought that our pain and pleasure are nothing until compared to others? If in any field I am better than someone else, I get pleasure. While someone else being better than me, gives me pain. When I compare myself with a poor man then I am contented thinking that I am rich compared to others. This satisfaction makes us relaxed but can further slowdown my growth rate. But when I compare myself with a rich man then it may be frustrating and may give me pain but this pain then motivates me to do smart work to be rich.

This is the pattern of thinking of an average person who has an average mindset. What I suggest is, just come out of this mindset of comparison. We can take the positive aspect of both the cases, that is, we feel happy for a rich person for his standard of living and get motivated, meanwhile, for better performance ourselves.

Your interest finds out your own style. Don't just think of walking upon the beaten path. Every great personality has their unique thoughts. They work upon their own ideas.

They work to expand their orbit gradually day by day. No great mind has ever lived without facing tough challenges and heart-breaking rejections initially. But ultimately they succeeded to convince the world with their own strong conviction. A strong conviction towards your own thoughts is a key factor which makes a man strong enough to keep him going.

- *Keep the process simple*
- *Keep the process continued*
- *Perfection and pleasure are gradual process*

It is very difficult to formulate one single reason which makes a man successful in his life, but impatient is certainly one single cause which makes a man unsuccessful in his life. Such an impatient mental attitude frequently changes his course of action and the direction of his action. This frequent changing action and direction reduces the resulting effect of his efforts. First we see that any process takes time to attain maturity and produce a fruitful result. This phenomenon is applicable to both right and wrong things. Everyone knows that morning walk is good for health, but walking for a few days or a week can't yield any appreciable effect on one's health. This is actually beneficial only when continued on regular basis. Until when it becomes a part of our life and it apparently demands no extra effort? Similarly, occasional consumption of alcohol may not have much adverse effect on one's health, but its regular consumption adversely affects our body gradually.

My simple idea is whatever you choose to do well or bad, it is fruitful only when it is done on a regular basis. Here is a story of a great saint Rumi. Rumi was very worried about his disciples they were very flicker minded. They did never stick to a particular method, and kept on changing their way of worship frequently. Guru Rumi understood the actual problem. He once took his disciples to a farmer who was digging a number of holes in search of water. The peculiar thing about it was that he was frequently changing the spot of digging the well. Every time he dug a few feet and then he moves to new hole when he do not get water. Then he would immediately switch to digging a new well at a new spot. Guru Rumi asked his disciples what was wrong with the farmer. They replied, to be impatient is the main problem of the farmer and he is changing his places frequently and that is the main reason why he couldn't get water even after so much effort. In this process, he has wasted a lot of his energy and time also; the field was filled with many small holes. In fact in this process the whole field was wasted while he couldn't get water.

Our efforts never pay us immediately; it takes a certain time for its maturity and give results. It is just like travelling to a particular destination, if we keep on changing our path frequently, we will never reach to our destination. Knowing or discovering the right path is very essential and it is a part of our travelling. Interestingly, if we use our time and energy in research only, we won't reach to our destination any way. There must be balance between research work and implementation. It is often found that a person involves himself only in research about the correct path then his ability to implement the information becomes weak and ineffective. Here a very important aspect of human nature works.

When our tendency in one area increases, it decreases in other areas. It is just like a flow of water, which has natural tendency to flow downward. It is a general rule that the path through which water flows becomes wider and deep day by day.

8.08 HIGHLIGHTS OF THIS CHAPTER

1. One right solution provides ten opportunities, while one wrong solution invites ten problems in life.
2. One small change in life becomes a big change in long run. A monkey started to walk on two feet and they converted into a man just due to a small technological change.
3. Expansion is a basic principle of life which gives pleasure of life. Gradual expansion makes anything easy and durable. British government came to India for trading, but gradually it took over the charge of the country, by expanding its territories one by one.
4. Technology expanded our capacities. Knife and swords are the expansion of nail. Terrestrial telescope is the expansion of human eyes. Computer is the expansion of our calculation power.
5. If you do not expand your capacity then capacity will decrease day by day. If we do not expand our territory then our territory will be attacked by external intruders. India's non-attacking image invited several external foreign attackers.
6. Just pick up a particular instrument or activity and develop mastery in that area and everything will be changed accordingly and be solved by solving only one thing in our life.
7. Raise your bar daily. This is just a basic like a mission statement of a high jumper, by which he enhances his performance on a daily basis. Go to extra mile is

same which helps us to expand our skill ability and performance day by day.

8. To be in a same orbit lifelong is quite a boring job just like a punishment. To be stagnating in any field is a punishment.
9. Keep the process simple and keep the process continue, perfection is a gradual process. Don't worry for the perfection but be worry for keeping the processes continue.

9. Success Is a Game

9.01 ONE RIGHT SOLUTION PROVIDES TEN OPPORTUNITIES

One right solution provides ten new opportunities

One wrong solution creates ten new problems

— *Chines Proverb*

We see a number of different people in our day to day life. The interesting thing is we found a person who developed in his life day by day while most are not developing in so speedy way. I analysed the actual reason behind this event. I noticed that the reason behind this success and failure was very simple. Most of the people have no interest in the solution of the problem and they apply very casual approach towards the solution of the problem. This casual approach to just finish the job creates a lot of problems later on. Unfinished job and imperfect work becomes more danger and attracts bigger problem. It is just like a chain reaction which attracts more problems one by one.

Failure of any type attracts more problem and failure, it is an established fact.

A boy came to city with his father. Here he got better environment from his village. His schooling happened in a better school and his life style became better. In this environment he decided to go to some different organizations as most used to opt the profession of guide.

His lifestyle became more comfortable and luxurious due to higher annual income. He could manage big bank balance and assets ethically due to his new job environment.

This life history reveals how he went to better environment and he got better opportunity. He availed the new opportunity and again he got bigger opportunity. When any solution is being done in better way many opportunities arise and it requires best use of the opportunities. In village the opportunity of schooling was not good that is why his father has decided to move to city where he was in service. His boy utilized the opportunity which he got at city. The opportunity developed since they had shifted to city. Better utilization of the opportunity again brings bigger opportunity and so on just like a chain reaction.

This is the reason why a person who becomes successful acquires more success day by day since every achievement provides ten more opportunities in his life. When a person fails, that failure brings in ten new problems, and makes a man difficult to come out of the series of failure. Suppose a person faces a big loss in his business. He becomes mentally upset and starts to take liquors. Gradually he becomes addicted to that and many health problem starts in his life along with the financial crises and loss of reputation in society. His life and his family life get worst affected due to the series of problems. It is absolutely true that any problem which comes into our life doesn't come alone. But, this fact is also true that any great solution brings a lot of solution in life.

It is very interesting that I have heard many times that "problem never comes alone" but just in a few instance I found that "solution also never comes alone." Many of us saw a student preparing very seriously for competitive examination. He did not get success in any. But all of sudden I heard that he got 3–4 offers from many commissions within a few months.

In day to day life, every person has to find solution for the problems. This solution is done by our whole-hearted efforts and many times half-heartedly efforts.

9.02 DEVELOPMENT OF SOCIETY

In ancient times, people started their life in forest. Their food and shelters were dependent on forest and water and transport requirements were fulfilled by river. This time people were living in a kabila [territory] for safety and folding, actually they all together hunt animals for food requirement. Thousands of years passed and humanity had crossed several milestones in their all-round developments like food, their shelter and communication. Dependency on other people has been defined and changed in many ways. The tribal life converted into society and feeling of togetherness decreased drastically. In tribal life, any problem to any member used to make concern to all the members. At that time the whole tribe was just like a big family which was headed by some senior and experienced member of tribe. This togetherness decreased time to time. Our area of concerned decreased day by day. After tribe and society, concept of joint family came. In which father, mother, many uncles, aunties and nephew all are members of a joint family. Every joy and sorrow equally affects each member of the joint family. The area of concern was all the family members of the joint family. Later on our society developed more and our area of concern decreased. The new concept emerged as the concept of nuclear family in which our concern is restricted among wife, husband and children.

It is very interesting to note that our area of concern decreased. It means our social feeling and bondage to other member of joint family and other person of our society has decreased. The contraction of area of concern has created many other social problems.

Of course we are living in a society but we all are living alone. That is why people living as neighbour don't know others. And their acquaintance is very formal. Now, visiting friends and neighbours are decreasing.

A large volume of mass people devote their time, energy and focus to religious activity due to their perception about great feeling towards the religious act. Great creative work will be done in country if their huge effort can be channelized for any constructive work in society for the welfare of society and mankind. The whole country will be changed within a short period.

9.03 SMALL PIECES OF ACHIEVEMENT BECOMES BIG ACHIEVEMENTS

It is great and most widely used technique to break in small pieces and to achieve one by one. From ancient times staircase and ladders are used to go to ground floor to first floor and upper floors. The steps of staircase is very good example which helps us to reach our goal to climb part by part. By crossing step by step we make ourselves climb high gradually and reach the next higher floor.

It gives a great truth of life that any big target can be achieved part by part. Even a child climbs to upper floor due to the staircase. Let us suppose I want to travel to New

Delhi by car which is a great attraction of tourist and it is our political capital too. Then two approaches can be adopted to reach destination. One approach may be filling our tank and food materials and starting our journey and trying to reach it in one span of journey. Just imagine how tension creating the journey it will be? Our vehicle may collapse, our driving capacity may collapse. Due to much tension, misshaping may occur. And it may be proved fatal to reach in one span of journey. Now the second option may be to break the journey into many small destinations. When we reach to our first destination on the path we feel relax and enjoy the journey. Human and the vehicle take proper break and rest. It is very important to increase our productivity to take a break during the journey. Our body regains its energy level for the next day move.

Every country has provided a weekly off, which refresh our energy and emotion which recharge us. When we take proper rest after proper time it becomes just an enjoyment since we see the new places and new things on the way. This process continues and we reach our destination enjoying the journey. In this process journey was not a task but it was an enjoyment.

Now let us see our everyday activities and we find that,

- Small achievements combines and become big achievement
- A small failure combines and becomes big failure

Have you ever noticed?

How we neglect our health issue every day and it grows a big health problem in a day?

How we postpone some urgent work daily and one day it becomes a great problem?

How we take care of our garden so that one day it develops into a beautiful garden?

How a person use smoking every day and his lung fails in medical report?

My simple view is our daily small creative and positive activity becomes a big achievement while our small harmful activity which we use to do daily how becomes a big failure?

Every day we put a lot of efforts towards our coveted goal. But we feel anxiety and irritation. Our performance and effort doesn't give us satisfaction for our further movement towards our goal. Despite our action and achievement we feel not satisfaction; the reason is very alarming and important to understand to grow up our pleasure and satisfaction.

Everyone is aware about the example of glass is half-filled or the glass is half-vacant. However there is another third dimension which says the glass is neither half-filled nor half-empty, but the glass is filled half with water and half with air. I want to discuss something how our mind thinks according to our statement?

When I say that glass is half-empty then immediately a picture comes in our mind that the glass is in process to being empty and it is now emptied half. According to our statement immediately a process appears in which it is to make empty. It indicates how our statement starts a process of thinking and action.

When I say that the glass is empty then immediately a picture comes in our mind the glass is being filled with water. Here the picture and process of thinking is just reverse to the empty statement. This is a great illustration about out tendency of work how it follows our statement and habitual way of seeing fact.

Now let us come to our feeling of dissatisfaction, which we feel daily while we do lot of works daily. The reason is very simple, we just think about what we could not do today. When we see the day such a way many things appear in front of us which was to be done. The dissatisfaction arises only due to our focus on unfinished things. This irritation can be reverse in easy way, if we could start to see the things what I have done today. Shifting our focus to the work done will change the way of our feeling and satisfaction. It is a matter of attitude and a way of thinking which makes us happy or unhappy.

Just start to think the today activity and think whatever I have done today is much more, I am satisfied very much. When we start to see our performance and feel that I have done today very much. This statement immediately creates a feeling of satisfaction.

When I ask my children that he is studying very well then a positive energy activates in his mind, and he put his more efforts in study. However, when parents condemn his lacking in study then a negative energy activates in his mind, which makes his study slow down. So positive feeling helps greatly to activate his positive energy, while negative statement and feeling activates his negative energy and slowdown his performance.

Everyone knows how appreciation enhances the performance of any child or any employee. I have a real life experience in which a boy became a mentally disturbed only due to his father's nagging behaviour towards him. His married life ruined completely and even now he is wandering to street and living his life by begging from people. I couldn't forget him life long since I had played cricket with him and know the fact that his father has ruined his life.

It is a very common tendency which is normally found in many parents to humiliate their children for their poor performance in examination. Parents are so much possessive towards their result in examination; they could not make them stop from scolding their ward. There is big misconception that he is enhancing his performance by humiliation. Many times it goes against his performance. In this process many child take immature steps even they commit suicide.

It is really a great responsibility of parents towards their children, which requires great patience and honest efforts for the right development of children. When parents become too much protective and give too much liberty to children both becomes harmful. Second thing over protection hampers the proper growth of children. Moreover, full liberty may put them on the wrong track. So parents have a great responsibility and it requires a constant watch about the right development and right activity.

9.04 LESSON FROM GARDENING

1. Start the process with very simple activity
2. Keep the process continue
3. Enjoy the process of gardening
4. You will so many plants, many will die while a few will grow
5. Your enjoyment will involve you more

6. Expertise will grow day by day, garden will grow more beautiful day by day

Just enjoy the process of gardening and your garden will expand qualitatively and quantitatively day by day. It is an automatic and just a gradual process.

The first requirement is to shift our focus to form a big and beautiful garden just enjoying the process of gardening. When we make a goal, then the gap between performance and goal creates no satisfaction in mind and the process becomes a boring job.

I have first chosen a plant which was capable to easily germinate in any pot. This way it started to give me great pleasure since the green plants were increasing in my garden. This is a very important lesson to start the process with easy way, which can be duplicable easily. I was not expecting for very beautiful flowers but I was enjoying my garden seeing it very green only. Another very important lesson is keeping your expectation low otherwise you may go in frustration. Day by day I have collected many plants from many places in a very gradual manner and my garden is growing in a very comfortable way.

The comfortable and easy growth is more stable.

I sowed many plants and seeds, a few of them grew up but many died. This process has given me a great lesson that every venture will not be a success. Despite many failures, a few will grow and that is enough. So don't be afraid with any failure, this is the part of learing. If any person is not failing in any means, then he is always moving on the beaten path. Such person will never be able to do something great in his life.

9.05 HIGHLIGHTS OF THIS CHAPTER

1. Success is nothing but a game. The more you learn and develop more skill you will enjoy the game more and more. This enjoyment will involve you in the game more and more.
2. Our area of concern contracting day by day. People were concerned for the tribe; later on our concern restricted to the members of joint family after that our concern restricted to wife, husband and for children only.
3. Any big journey is completed by completion of small destination. Breaking up the goals into small goals is the easiest method to accomplishment of big goal. Part by part a man can eat even an elephant.
4. Gardening is just like an open book which teaches great things. Just enjoy the process of gardening, automatically it will expand day by day and it will be more enjoying.
5. You will start many ventures and many of them may fail but by this process you will find out the real project most suitable to you.

10. Challenges Develop

10.01PIGEONSAND THEIR STRUGGLE

I used to see every day a dozen of pigeons come at a particular palace in search of food grains. They don't get sufficient food grains required for such number. It has to go to many particular places in expectation of sufficient food. Every day they have to wander many palaces for the search of foods. Every day they have to face many challenges and struggle for their food, nest and their survival. On the other hand, my son is keeping four love birds in a cage and is providing them sufficient food grains and water. They don't have to face any struggle for food, water and shelter. They don't have any problem for their survival too.

Now I compare the effect of struggle in their life. The life of pigeons is filled with struggle and challenges whereas the four love birds are completely free from these challenges and threat. The effect can be very distinctly observed. The pigeon's life is very energetic, very alert and enjoying free movement in their life. There is a glazing in its wings and very strong wing. On other hand, the four love birds are very dull. Every day they have the same food at same time without any struggle. The very specific thing is there is no charm and excitement on their face. Although it has secure food and shelter, it has lost freedom in his life. And another interesting thing I found that one of the four birds got an opportunity to escape but it returned back to the cage next day since it has lost the ability to struggle for food and the skill to keep him alive in this world.

Most of us want to live a very safe and secure life but we don't know what we are losing in this process. We don't realize that how uncertainty helps us to fill enthusiasm and essential factor for the growth of life. Challenges make a man smart and stronger. And the routine life gradually becomes very dull and charmless.

Challenges and struggles make our mind fresh and energetic.

Every one of us wants a comfortable and joyful life. Most of the person doesn't like challenges and difficulties. They think it is a painful and unnecessary thing for our life, that's why most of them avoid and want to escape the challenges. However they don't realize the real use and necessity of the challenges in our life. Our pleasure and happiness are directly related to challenges. The value of any achievement is determined by the magnitude of challenges which the winner had overcome and achieved the desired level. Suppose you go to a bookstall and see two books are displayed in the dashboard. One is the life of Dhirubhai Ambani and another book is life of Mukesh Ambani. Which book will you choose to purchase? Obviously, you will choose the book of Dhirubhai Ambani. Why the book has so appeal against the life of Mukesh. A very important aspect that is "challenge" is missing in the life is Mukesh. Since, he had not to face the challenges in his life that is why his is life is no interesting. Dhirubhai is a best example of a person who becomes a hero from zero.

Any movie becomes blockbusters is a story of a hero who overcomes huge challenges. The skill and ability to overcome the challenges and to accomplish his goal to destroy the enemy of mankind creates a great appeal in mass people. Film producer makes such film which satisfies the psychological need of mass people. That is why he creates such difficult situation, almost impossible to overcome. And the hero overcomes these challenges by his intelligence, courage and fighting skills. The capability to overcome makes audience mad. Individual has no capability to do so, but he makes himself satisfy by seeing these impossible performances of the hero.

Normally, people avoid taking risk, they avoid pain. But development and growth both are associated with an ability to take risk and ability to bear pain. When we avoid challenges in our life actually it increases challenges in life.

Most of our young generation don't want to take pain to get up early and they don't want to take the pain of morning walk. This behaviour develops a lot of health problem in later age which makes their life miserable.

When a man says that a situation is very difficult, it indicates how he is thinking about the situation. It is not concerned with the difficulties but it is the attitude which is not taking a chance to handle the situation. The same situation can be handled by other person very easily. Basically it is the problem of his mindset.

He can't accept his incapability, lacking his skill and confidence. But his ego does not accept his lacking. Acceptance of the problem is the first step towards the solution and development. Everywhere people who are not skilled always condemn the computer. To accept incapability requires very high moral values and strong desire to make them skilful and efficient.

Challenges can be treated as a problem or as an opportunity. Challenges are just an opportunity to develop our skill and ability. If we use the challenges on right way then we can enhance our personality. Any defence personnel have to undergo compulsorily a rigorous physical training programme designed by defence. This rigorous training programme makes defence personnel tough, skilled and capable to handle any difficult situation further in his job assignment.

"Either you fight against the challenges

Or, you flight from the challenges"

When challenges come on our life there are only two ways of dealing. Either we can fight or we can flight. When we fight and overcome the challenges then our skill, efficiency and confidence grows up. But when we escape, our skill, efficiency and confidence decrease from its existing level.

Challenges make a man stronger, smarter and tough.

Just develop an attitude to "Do Difficult Job"

10.02 HOW A SMALL SHARK KEEPS THE FISH FRESH

Japan is a big fish producing and fish exporting country in the world. They travel a long distance from coast for fishing in the sea. They come back to coast which takes 1–2 days normally. The fish won't remain fresh after such a gap from fishing to till they reach the fish market. They made a fish tank on the ship where they kept the fish in tank and it reaches fresh to the market. But in the tank too, the fish remained dull and it doesn't remain like a fresh fish. This way the demand and pricing both were decreasing day by day. The fish producing company were very worried about this problem. Suddenly they found a very unique and very cheaper solution for this problem. They put a small shark in the fish tank. This shark keeps all the fish in movement round the clock, since it keeps on running in the fish tank to keep them safe from the shark. This method worked and the entire fish remained fresh due to hectic movement for saving their life risk from the small shark.

They find a very interesting solution to keep the fish fresh even in a fish tank. Without any risk and challenge our life becomes dull. An excitement is a very essential part of liveliness of life. Growth happens in our life only when we handle the challenging situation. Challenges provide opportunity for growth of our personality. It develops our skill, efficiency and our smartness.

"Gardening is a gradual process

Don't worry for perfection

Worry for continuation

Perfection is a gradual and automatic process."

"Our action and ability speak louder than voice."

10.03 LESSON FROM KITE FLYING

In a season of kite fly, I saw many boys running holding the thread in their hand for the take-off of their kite. Among them, Sonu was also making consistent effort for the take-off of his kite. After many failures, he examined the angle of the kite made some changes by adjusting the knot and he again started to run for the take-off of his kite. This time the angle of the kite was right and kite started to rise in the air. He started to screech with joy since his effort became successful and his kite was raising high and high. Now he realizes that it is rising in the air automatically and no efforts are required to keep it high. He was very surprised by this phenomenon. Sonu called his father in a very joyous mood and he described how all his several efforts failed and how a small adjustment in its angle of kite succeeded to fly so easily.

His father said there is a great lesson you can learn from this failure and success. Your many efforts initially failed. But failure doesn't mean that it went in vain. This failure has given you an insight to re think about the actual problem, and by the trial and error method ultimately you have found the right solution and after necessary changes your kite have started to fly in an easy manner. Later on you realize that there is no need to put any effort to keep the kite flying. Since it has reached to the upper level of flowing wind and now you need not to do any effort to keep it flying.

This phenomenon is applicable not only to kite but all of our venture and even for a student who doesn't feel interested in his studies due to his initial failure in studies. But a sincere student by his commitment and consistent efforts analyses the process of his studies and makes changes in the process and his success level increase. As his rate of success increases in study, his achievements become a great motivating factor which keep him focused in his study. Now it becomes difficult to involve these students in other activities other than their studies.

Any new project is a bit difficult to survive in any venture since the rate of achievement is very low at the starting stage since the person is new and he commits several mistakes during the process. These mistakes are properly analysed and the method of work improves accordingly, and thus success rates also improve gradually.

Conclusion: At starting stage rate of success is low and many failure happens and it is difficult to survive. But those who modify their process of work gradually overcome the initial failure and start to achieve bigger goal day by day.

Now Sonu was enjoying kite flying with his father. The wind was smooth and the kite was flying very high. The thread was in the hand of the children, and he was very much thrilled for kite flying. Suddenly the child realizes that the kite would go to the sky, if it is allowed freely to fly. He asked his father, about his idea to cut the thread. His father asked him that you are thinking that thread is an obstacle in flying to the sky. But you don't know the thread is a support by which it is flying so high. Child got confused with the reply of his father. Father realized that he has not taken his point, so he decided to explain his idea to his child by demonstration. He allows his son to cut the thread. As the thread was separated, the kite immediately started to fall down and within a few second, it came down to the earth. His son was looking the falling of the kite and bewildered when unable to explain the falling. He saw his father with a curiosity. Father explained that thread was a support by which the kite was flying at so height. As this support is withdrawn, immediately it falls down to the earth. You are unable to understand that which you are looking as bondage is actually a support which makes a kite to fly so high.

The children hugged his father with tears and said to his father to forgive him since he was annoyed with his father's restriction imposed to him. Now he realized his father's restriction was not against him, but it was an invisible supporting hand which was helping and protecting even when he is away from his father.

10.04 LOVING CHILDREN

The basic question is how anybody can change their life? As we know that our normal tendency plays a vital role in guiding and monitoring our life and our behaviour. If we change our normal tendencies and pattern of behaviour, we can change our destiny and our life. This is a fact that pleasure is a very important thing which makes us more involved in any activity. But in initial stage, activity doesn't be a joyful activity. It is just like mathematics. For normal students mathematics is a difficult subject but who has practices and developed efficiency in mathematics, they actually enjoy mathematics. It is a fact that it is interesting for those who have developed sufficient efficiency in the subject.

Just like mathematics any area becomes enjoying when we develop our skill and efficiency up to a certain level. The phase when we start anything and our skill has not developed up to a certain level is very difficult to sustain in the process. Most of the people quit in this stage. This stage is like an infant child who has no capacity to face any adverse situation; it is fully dependent to its parent.

Just think of a new born child which is delicate. It requires constant care by its parent. Such new born child requires 24 hour care for its right growth and for its survival too. Every parent pays their constant care to such a new born baby. The baby grows day by day and the required care decreases gradually. And a time comes when it is grownup sufficiently to look after his requirement. Later on it grows so sufficient that he can take care of himself including his parents and his children. Not only this, but he runs a big organization by his ability and efficiency.

It simply shows that any idea which we accept must be cared like an infant child. Suppose one wants to be a wildlife photographer then he has to protect his desire just like a child. Our constant care and protection of this desire will become stronger day by day like a child. Later on it will grow sufficient and will be able to control all other things of our life. As we know that child doesn't give us anything in return at the early stage but we take care constantly due to our love towards the children. Every parent pays utmost care to their children not due to any hope for return but due to their love. It is another thing that when the child grows up completely, expectation develops in the mind of his parent. On his complete growth he returns back much time bigger to his parent. When a parent takes care of their children for the future return then the beauty of the affection is lost. It becomes just an investment not love. When we care our children for love, then the level of the beauty is quite different.

Suppose I choose dancing as my career and I dance only in expectation for great reward and recognition then the beauty of dancing is lost. Act of dancing due to love for dancing is really great. The class and quality are different due to our love for dancing.

Whatever we choose as a goal in our life, don't expect much from this goal but just love your goal and enjoy. This love will pay your right effort to the activities required for achieving your goal.

10.05 QUALITY OF LIFE

Everyone lives his life either as a poor or rich, either a successful man or failed man. But the main question is whether they are living a quality life or they are just living a burden of life. Many of the people are living since they couldn't die. Often we have experienced that a fly wants to go out from a window but it collides with the glass and fails. It makes several attempts to go out, but fails and the most interesting thing that there is another window is open and it may go out very easily through another window. It wastes a lot of energy and time to go out but it is obvious that it is not possible to break the window glass.

Our life is just like a fly which is completely focused that our pleasure is possible only by getting power, position or money. We are unable to think that there is also many other ways by which we can make our life happy and joyful. What is the basic reason behind this approach?

An average people always follow the average path which most of the people follows. An average people always follow the beaten path.

Extraordinary people always follow the extraordinary path for their desired goal.

This is just an approach of a man who has a tendency to do something new and to do something different. His mind always thinks something new and something great.

"I want to hire a lazy man in my company since due to his laziness he always finds some unique and easy solution for any work for his laziness."

–Bill Gates

This is a tendency which keeps the mind of a few people involved to find out some unique solution, some unique way to do a particular job. All new discoveries happened in this world only due to those people who have not followed the beaten path. All the new countries have been discovered and new researches happened only due to those people who had dared and acted. They are not satisfied with the present situation only. Their mind and thinking always involve in the search for new solution. These are the people who have always given new solution and new path for the whole world to follow make their life easy.

New search always involve a risk of failure and many other risk which a normal person avoid. He has a normal tendency to avoid risk that is why they follow only the tested method. But there are people who enjoy taking risk. Really those are just like a see diver who dive into a sea and find out pearls for the world. Rest of the world just sit beside the sea and clap on the achievement of the sea divers.

Of course risk and pain always involve but this is also a fact that, this risk and pain makes our achievement more joyful.

So, the whole world is grouped as a small number of people who dare and perform while others clap on the performance.

10.06 PARENTS RESPONSIBILITY

If a child steals money from his home then his parent is certainly responsible for his a tendency. Personality formation is process which depends on his home enviournment, his enviournment where he grown up and the educational institution where he got education. No parent can escape from his responsibility if a child becomes a criminal. When a child becomes successful in his life than parent takes responsibility for his success then obviously he will be held responsible if a child fail to be a good citizen of our country.

But This is a very simple example how our human nature takes credit for what happens great in life while he escapes from the responsibility if happens something wrong in his life or to his children.

When any cricket match happens in India then suddenly it seems that the level of patriotism level grows all of sudden everybody talks and becomes concern for the victory of his nation. All of these vanishes all of sudden. If India loosed the game then every person becomes an expert of the cricket. Many blame that our team loses only due to lacking of team work. We expect that they must have a great team spirit, only which makes our team winner. Any individual must ask with himself that is he working in his organisation with a team spirit? Is he living in his society with a team spirit?

We are just an expert commentator and keep on commentary on other's performance. Those who are not so capable have too much expectations from others.

Our expectation is prime factor which decide our motivation level. But the question is how our motivation level related to our expectations. By example we clarify how high level of expectation decrease our motivate level and our performance.

Suppose a student decide to solve 100 sums in a particular day. He will realise the feeling of achievement when he completes 100 questions. For this big achievement he has to work hard and in this process frustration may develop in his mind which will de motivate from the action. Most of the frustration develops in life only due to our high level of expectation. But think about that if a student decide to solve only 10 sum instead of 100 sums then this level can be achieve by a little effort and a feeling of achievement develops in his mind. The feeling of achievement gives a mental satisfaction and recharges our desire to do more for more achievement. This feeling of achievement develops a feeling of enthusiasm and motivates more for more achievement. Such feeling makes great changes in level of involvement in the activity to acquire more achievement.

To set higher goal is basically due to our impatient mindset which wants to achieve more in short time. Most of us do not understand how, due to wrong mental attitude we lost our motivation level. Every parent has complain that his son or daughter don't devote his much time in study. This is a very common problem about the lacking interest in study but it is the basic problem of motivation level due to high expectation level of parent and students toward his study.

We understand how our high expectation reduces our motivation level and our involvement decreases in the process and it is discontinued. So the right attitude is to reduce your expectation level to maintain high level of achievement rate which will increase our involvement in the activity. The activity may be anything including study also.

10.07 HIGHLIGHTS OF THIS CHAPTER

1. Challenges are just a filtering arrangement which filters out the winners from the mass people. Winners like challenges since it provides opportunity to develop their skill and efficiency to go ahead despite of all the challenges and adverse.
2. Most of the people are living in a hidden prison build by their own perception and their belief.
3. Pleasure is deeply associated with challenges. So if there are no challenges in the life then there is no pleasure in life.
4. Without challenges life becomes dull and without enthusiasm. A diamond gets its actual value, only when it is grinded and polished by grinding machine.
5. Kite fly higher in the air against the flow of the wind. It means that real hero raises high in adverse situation.
6. A person who has a clear vision and strong reason moves always towards his goal despite of all the challenges.
7. Parents take care for their children in love, without love it becomes just as an investment.
8. Just a few people dare and perform while rest of the world clap on the performance.
9. Higher expectation level reduces our level of motivation and achievements. Lower expectation increases our involvement and achievements.

11. Time Management

11.01 TIME MANAGEMENT

Now a day it is a very common excuse that "He has no time." What does it mean? This statement is not a problem but it indicates that he is lacking in ability to manage time. Many friends used to say that he has no time to spare time to meet friends. On an average people spend his minimum 2–3 hours before the TV. But he complains that he has no time. If a person says that he couldn't meet my friend due to lack of time that means his friend is very lower in his priority list. Every person has his own priority list it may be written or unwritten. What is in his top priority is very important which is decided by his attitude and his real priority in his life.

Our priority in our life determines our way of thinking and our daily activities. Suppose a boy has a strong vision to be a great cricketer in his life then he we do everything which requires being a great cricketer. Other activities will be given less priority in comparison to the regular practice of cricket. A student has dream to crack IIT JEE then his whole activates will be arranges accordingly.

It is important that if we have some great vision in your life then there will be no room for unnecessary activity. But if one has no big priority in his life then he will make many useless things in his life as if they are very great things. I have one friend who loves his pet very much. There is nothing bad in loving his pet. But if one pays his too much attention to his beloved pet then he will not have any spare time to do some other great things in his life. Many scientists had not married in their life, only due to his so much involvement in his creative work. He was so much involved in his project that never realized to marry in his life and remained unmarried whole life.

If any garden is not used for growing valuable plants then unwanted plants will grow up automatically. And second thing if the unwanted plants are not removed on a regular basis, it will hamper the growth of valuable plants.

Time management is nothing but it is just managing us according to the time. The busiest person has more spare time since he know how to manage time. We are very careful in spending our money which is our hard earned. But we don't care for how we are wasting our time. The most important thing is we don't get it back the wasted time. Every day we waste a lot of time. Still we are not so aware like our awareness of spending our money.

Why we don't care for wasting our time? To understand this cause first we have to understand why everyone is so aware about spending his money? Earning of money is not free like the time. We have to do some work or some investment against which we earn money since we earn money by effort that adds value to money. Money does not come in our life without any effort that is why everyone pays so much care in spending their money. Even a person who earns money by illegal and unfair means pays so much care in spending money. So the fact is that how we earn anything that adds value in money.

People used to talk that the guava which they steal from other's garden involves a lot of risk and thrill. These guavas give much taste in comparison to the guava which we brought from the market by purchasing. Value and taste are added by how we have acquired the fruits. A person purchases one bottle of drinking water in train by paying twenty rupees. He drinks the water completely before the journey is completed since he had paid money for that. But the water which he had taken from his home, which is free, he throws the water on completion of the journey. On throwing he doesn't feel any hesitation since he had not paid twenty rupees for this water.

Money which is spent can be earned again, but the time wasted can't be backed again. But we pay much value to money since we have paid something to earn money but we don't give much importance to our time since we all are getting it free, without any efforts.

Time management is nothing but it is just priorities in our works. It is basically distinguished between essential and non-essential jobs. Everybody is given twenty four hours. There is no injustice by nature to everybody. In fact nature never does any injustice to anyone. It is just our explanation and our excuse that nature had injustice with me. They equally give twenty four hours. It is very important that how we utilize this given period.

By careful analysis of twenty-four hours how it is utilized, it is found that average and below average people mostly accommodate unnecessary works within twenty-four hours, due to lack in priority. They spend their twenty-four hours for unnecessary works. And hardly, he does the necessary works during the hours. On the other hand the successful person accommodates his most essential works first in his available twenty-four hours and non-essential jobs are hardly accommodated.

Successful people | **Unsuccessful people**

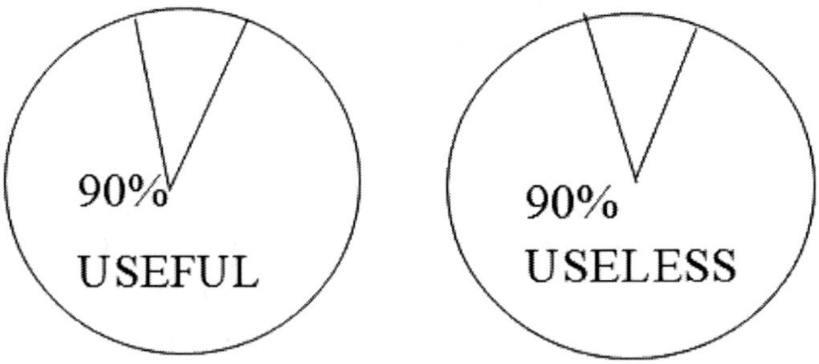

90% time goes to essential works | **90% of time goes to non-essential works**

This is the basic problem which makes a man successful and failed. Actually the failed people have no control over their activities. They just do what their mind asks to do for immediate pleasure. They are unable to think on the basis of long run effect.

Successful people arrange all their activities according to their valuable goals. Their action and priority are decided by their valuable goal. Their activities are chosen on the basis of long run effect which is helpful in their long term goal which has been decided by them.

Time management is just an art to fruitful management of our available resources in which "time" is also a very important component of them.

11.02 MANAGEMENT SKILL

A sailor sails his boat in a river. He has no control over the flow of wind. Inexperienced sailor always condemns the flow of wind since it is not always favourable for the movement of the boat. But an experienced sailor never condemns the wind. He knows that there is nothing to condemn the wind, in spite to practice and make adjustment with the wind. Flow of wind is a natural phenomenon. We can't make change anything in this event, so complaining about the flow of wind is worthless. In spite, we learn and adjust our sail according to the direction of the wind. The only important thing is how to use the power of wind in moving ahead our boat. If the wind is completely in the opposite direction then how can we minimize the adverse effect of the wind? This is a most important skill which is needed to learn and practice.

Adjustment of our sail is the adjustment with the natural things to use it in favourable ways or to minimize its adverse effect.

In 2004, our Tamil Nadu, Andhra Pradesh coastal area were mostly damaged by Tsunami caused by an earthquake at Indonesia. I fortunately I witnessed the worse hit at Marina Beach at Chennai. When the high tide due to Tsunami backed, it washed out all the shops on the Marina Beach. Many casualties happened in this Tsunami high tide. I noticed a very interesting thing at the beach which taught us a great lesson about life against the worse natural calamity. A number of cut-outs made by plywood of actors and actress were kept on the sand. Tourist used to get photograph with the actors and actress on the sea beach. I noticed that all the shops and cut-out were washed out in the Tsunami except one wooden cut-out. I noticed and started to think how this single cut-out remained on its place while of others washed out with the misty waves. The reason was very simple since the cut-out was a piece of thin plywood which thickness was hardly three millimetres was placed in 180 degree south direction of the wave. It fortunately placed in just in the same direction with the direction of the wave. That is why the wave applied its minimum force on the ply board and it remained in standing position as usual.

What is our angle is very important which affects our life against any adverse situation of life.

Coaches know always more techniques comparatively to the player, although the player always gets many hundred times more name fame and recognitions. Although, a player works according to the guidance of his coach, he has skill and ability to implement. Coach knows only the technique but it is the player who learns and practices the technique in playing for high score. To develop an ability to implement is the key factor which pays more reward and recognitions to the players. To know the right techniques is just a mental process in which one reads a book of a particular game but to develop this skill is not just a mental activity but it is an active process of learning on regular basis by which a particular skill is conveyed to the subconscious mind of the player. It requires constant mental and physical involvement and practice. This shows that to know anything is not so important than to implement. Capability to implement is a great thing.

What you want to be in life just start to develop a mindset of such personality.

This book doesn't claim that it will give you some magic tricks or magic formula which will change your life overnight or within one week or two weeks. I don't believe in such things. Life doesn't change in such a manner. Otherwise anyone can change their life in magical ways since a number of books are available in the market which claims to change our life within a week.

I visualize that changing of life is an active process which happens gradually. It doesn't means that life cannot be changed within overnight. Our perception and pattern of thinking may change overnight by any incident. Our behaviour, way of dealing and test other things will follow accordingly.

Any change happens in our life when a burning desire develops in our mind to do something. Just not to remain same as usual. If a burning desire starts in the mind of any reader then he will start to find out the way to change his life. This will create an inner unrest in mind and body. Nothing will remain without changing.

A good person gives pleasure, while a bad person gives experience which makes us strong, smart and skilled. So never try to escape from bad people or bad situations. Actually they provide an opportunity to develop our skills and efficiency. Our development is always associated with challenging works. So face the challenges. It must be entered in our subconscious mind.

An experienced share broker always gets benefit from the up and down trends of the share market. He doesn't become panic when market falls, he just do what is best suitable to do when market is falling. It is worthless to shout about the falling of the market. It is not in my control.

So it is necessary to focus on the things which is in our control, and need to do that only. Most of the successful people focus on the things which are in their control. Most of the average and mediocre people make shouting about fall of market. They will do big discussion about political discussion, in which they have no much control over it.

When people and critics criticize or appreciate the performance of Tendulkar, he keeps himself busy in practicing the batting technique. He knows very well that his performance will only be the best reply to the people. It is not very effective to give them reply verbally. It is the Tendulkar who got so respect and appreciation worldwide, since he knows well what to do and the most important quality is he has the capability to do what he ought to do.

11.03 COMMITTING MISTAKE IS A PART OF LEARNING

"Either you win or you learn."

Failure isn't failure unless you don't learn from it.

—Dr. Ronald Niednagel

We purchase TV set and it comes with a manual book in which instructions are given for the method of use. But in life manual book is not available by which we can use it properly. We have to learn it by the experiences from others and by self-experiences. Life is just an open book from which we have to learn every day. God has given liberty to choose everybody from the large options. But it doesn't mean they have should have wisdom to choose right things. This liberty to choose according to his choice many times causes a lot of problem due to inability to choose right things. Lack of ability to choose right things creates great problem in life.

"Everybody has liberty to choose according to his choice.

Everybody has no wisdom, what to choose right for him."

It is everybody is given a lot of option in their life and he is independent to choose any of them. But the huge option becomes a cause of problem too. There huge option increases the chances of committing mistake in any action. Huge options freedom to choose them causes great problems in life too. Most of us commit mistake due to a large number of options.

We understand the actual reason of mistake. Thus we will have to apply trial and error method to choose the right option among the available options.

Remember the stage when a child tries to stand up and fall many times.

11.04 DIFFERENT SKILLS REQUIRED

Every defence personal has to undergo compulsorily a basic physical training which makes them capable to meet them their job assignments. Apart from the physical exercise, they have to acquire a number of different skills which help them to perform their duty.

- Discipline and punctuality
- Daily physical training makes immediate action on command
- Mountain climbing

- Practice of shooting on target
- Survival strategy in adverse situation

A motor mechanic uses different tools for opening and fitting the different components of engine. One tool will not be able to open at all the places. Similarly a human being requires different skills and ability to successfully handle every situation and make him capable to go ahead towards goal in all the situations. A few examples are as follows.

- Determination
- Commitment
- Pain-bearing capacity
- Skill in marketing
- Computer skill and efficiency

11.05 HORSE RIDER ADJUSTS HIS MOVEMENT WITH THE HORSE

It is very interesting to see how a horse rider makes his body moves according to movement of a horse. Why he doesn't sit quietly on the back of horse? This is a very important thing which helps to increase the speed of the horse. Not only it increases the speed of the horse, but it minimizes the jerks and shocks which are created by the fast movement of horse.

Even a cycle rider always adjusts his body movement according to the movement of a cycle. This body adjustment helps him to keep the cycle balanced and move fast.

11.06 HIGHLIGHTS OF THIS CHAPTER

1. People who complain that they have no time don't mean that they have no time but they have no priority

in their life. If you are not managing time then you will be managed by time.

2. People say it time management but in fact you have to manage yourself according to the time.
3. Most of the people don't give much value to the time since it is available free to everybody. We have a mental attitude to give value only those things in which money is involved by any means.
4. Management of time is just like a management skill which requires practicing consistently and we develop mastery in time management gradually.
5. Aligning our self is a great management skill which develops our proficiency and efficiency. It is just like a horse rider who makes his body movement according to the motion of the horse.
6. A child develops his ability to align his body with the gravitational force and later on to keep him balanced becomes a natural habit and his subconscious mind takes care to keep him balanced in every moment.

12. Millionaire's Mindset

12.01 PERCEPTION OF POOR MINDSET

It is very clear that a poor man is poor since he has a very strong belief in his mind that money earning is a very difficult thing. We have shortlisted some common perceptions which are generally found in the mind of a poor man.

- Earning money is very difficult thing
- Accumulation of earning wealth is not possible without illegal activity
- I hate money
- I am not a lucky man to be rich
- They suffer from fear psychosis for losing money and never invest for big returns
- I have no family background so that I can be a rich man

These are just a few perceptions which are generally found in the mind of poor people. The interesting thing is he lives with such poor people who also have the same feeling. All of them have same mental belief which helps others to make their wrong mental belief stronger. Never a question arises in his mind that he may be wrong? His pattern of thinking may be incorrect? Mass appeal is very strong and effective. He thinks that all are thinking just like me. Many people thinking like the same may not be incorrect. This is a big example of mutual deception, all are making other's wrong perception strong and that becomes their destiny.

Then what is the way to change our perception. It is very difficult and very easy also. First we have to change our way of thinking, but it is not possible if we keep associated with the same people. We have to first change our association and to associate with such people who are earning huge since their perception towards money is different.

Any changes start in life from changing our process of thinking and process of belief. Only our activity and behaviour will change accordingly.

12.02 PERCEPTION OF RICH MAN

Money is nothing but just a mental belief. It is just a display of our mental pattern of thinking and our belief. They knowingly and unknowingly adopt many techniques which attracts huge money in their life. The first and most important thing which makes them rich is their passion for wealth. Now I list down the prime factors which attract wealth in life.

- They love money and are passionate about that
- They have only one feeling about money to acquire money more and more
- They are not fearful for losing money, that's why they make investment for higher returns
- They never condemn those who have wealth

There is a very basic difference between accumulation of money and actual wealth. Merely accumulation of money doesn't bring peace in life. Money is acquired by lot of means in which legal and illegal ways are used. Of course, accumulation of money gives luxuries in life but it doesn't give real happiness and peace of mind if it is accumulated by unfair means. Money acquired by unfair means gives lot of powers and luxuries but at the same time our peace of mind is lost and we live in a shadow of legal complication in many ways. A fearful mindset develops, and in many case earned money, name and fame all are lost due to illegal earning of money.

Most of the people get trapped in a number game in concern of money matter. Their greed for earning money grows more and more as he becomes expert in the game of money earning. Their greed becomes so hostile and they don't bother whether the means is right or wrong.

Lower moral value + high earning money= makes greedy

High moral value + high earning money = makes generous.

When a man becomes greedy then his greed for earning money becomes a never ending process. He adopts all the unethical and illegal means to earn money. A few doctors are found in society who is very noble by the profession, but their mindsets are worse than even a kidnapper type criminal since they blackmail patients for money, saying that their life is under risk. They are using their noble profession for blackmailing and earning huge money.

Earning money for normal requirement is fulfilled, but greed for money is never satisfied.

In this world, all the people have their own world in their mind. They have different requirement for pleasure. Some becomes happy with his latest model car; some feels happy with his imposing home like this. One of my friends has great fond of depositing money in his bank account. He said that a big amount printed in his pass book gives him great pleasure. His satisfaction is connected to the feeling that I have accumulated such a huge amount. He will feel a pain, if he has to spend any amount from this account.

His son aged twenty-eight years got arrear rupees 30,000 rupees on his wages revision. He suggested him to get fixed deposit in banks so that it will be 60,000 rupees in six years and it will be 1,20,000 rupees in the next six years. By this way your money will grow from 30,000 to 1,20,000 rupees within a period of twelve years. His son was planning buy a motor bike which cost was nearly 35,000rupees at that time. He replied to his father that of course 30,000 rupees will become, 1,20,000 rupees in twelve years but my life will be lapsed without having a motor cycle. Without motor cycle I will not be able to do proper movement which required for all-round development of my life and career. And secondly the purchasing power of 1,20,000 rupees after twelve years will reduced to just 40,000 rupee in comparison to today. His father was not convinced since his miser mind is filled with a fear from investing money.

He purchased a two wheeler bike as it was his dream. This bike enabled him to speed the movement and made him capable to manage many big things which were almost impossible to do without a vehicle. He purchased a plot and constructed his dream house simultaneously with his regular service. Till date he never realized how this investment in bike made him capable to do so many jobs in so early stage of his life.

It is important to stand boldly for your point of view. You may have to face the opposition of your father too, but you must have the courage to stand by your point of view, if it is right.

It is a very common fact that before 20–30years back, many people had taken their third or fourth issue only under compulsion of their parents. They can't oppose them and his family became comparatively bigger and lifelong he has a guilt feeling for his big family size. Many people have no long vision, but if you have a real correct vision then you must have a capacity to stand with your view.

When you work according to your vision and plan initially, you have to face much opposition from your family members and from external people. This is a testing time which you have to overcome and prove how strong your commitment for your belief is. This foremost condition and initial signal show how you are strong enough to stand alone against all the adverse.

Such fearful mind always prefers to deposit money in bank for his safe but slow growth. His mind never allows him to invest money for better returns in other areas. Earning money is also related to the risk-bearing capacity and capacity to invest is a big factor in any venture.

A very famous quote is

"A ship is safer in a dockyard, but it is not meant for that." Similarly, "Money is safer in bank but it is not meant for that."

An employee also thinks different methods of investment for his money growth. But he doesn't dare to think outside the box. He will think like recurring deposit schemes, deposit in PPF account or extra deposit in his voluntary PF account. He will think always in this area only.

He has a general attitude to suggest his close relative and friend to make systematic investment in secure scheme, by curtailment in many requirement of day to day requirement of his life. To minimize his daily requirement is also a very important strategy for his financial strategy.

Over protection of money decreases its efficiency just like over protection of any child hampers the growth of a child. Money is just like a blood of market, and it must keep on flowing then only the market is said to be alive. The flow of blood in a young man is fast while it becomes slow in the blood vessels of old man. When the flow of blood stops in any part of the body it clots and creates many diseases. When water keeps on flowing in a river, it is fresh but when it is kept in a pond, in absence of flow in water, it becomes contaminated. Flow is a very essential factor for the freshness of water. Fresh water gives life to the human being, animals and plants.

Flow of money is very essential in life just like blood and water. Those who want to choke this flow either money or blood many problem starts in life. In practical business, we see that if any goods are not in sale then it is better to sell out even at the lower cost to its purchasing cost. The concept behind this, this is good to choke the flow of money. Immature shopkeeper holds it in the expectation for selling with profit, but he doesn't notice how this good is choking the fund flows, which is a great damage for the business process. The basic fact is to release the fund to invest in other goods for rotation of money.

Rotation of money is the main component by which money multiplies. In which market rotation of money is very fast, there the growth of money becomes fast. In which market rotation is fast that market is considered more live market and people prefer to do their business in such market.

How you earn money is a most important factor which decide the effect of this money in your life. Money earned with ethics and values create happiness and peace in life. This is called real wealth.

Illegal money or money which is compromised with values and principles brings fear and unrest in life. It is just like you have all luxuries but you don't feel enjoyment for your wealth. Illegal earning doesn't pollute your life only but it pollutes your generation also. I have found in many cases where father gained huge money and his son became a bigger money multiplier by illegal ways.

Another great problem for such people, they develop such a mindset to assess people on the basis of their bank balance. They have no valuable thing except money. Their money power makes them fanatic that they feel they can buy anything by the power of money. They think moral values are meaningless things, since they can get their work done through any person by the power of money.

12.03 MILLIONAIRE'S MINDSET

A latest survey report published, which is very interesting and it makes our belief very strong that wealth is just a mindset.

1% People holds99% of the wealth of whole world

Only 62%people hold 50% of the wealth of whole world

Every millionaire is a leader. They understand that they must follow great leaders as they become one. They know when to take responsibility and initiative when tough situations occur. When testing time comes, they pass the test and assure others in a positive way that they are in good hands. A mark of a true leader inspires others that they can do the unimaginable.

Millionaires understand that the secret of living is giving. Many wealthy people give relentlessly. You can only be wealthy by enhancing the wealth of others. However, when it comes to charity, they don't just drop a check in the pile like most people do. Instead, they actually participate by knowing exactly where the money is going.

Millionaires send out thousands of emails every year. Every email builds your brand. They are also specialists on the phone and meeting face to face. The more effectively you can share your message with the world, the more likely people will want to work with you. The level of your communication will determine the level of your wealth.

Building relationships is instrumental in the world of business. You must be a reliable source in order to attract reliable sources. In my network, I have every conceivable skill available. It's only a phone call or email away. The only way you can get big things done is by employing those who can do the things that you cannot (or don't want to) do. The people you're looking for are also looking for you.

If you can take care of yourself, you can take care of thousands of people. Knowing human nature is the key to success. Millionaires understand motivation, body language, tone of voice, tact, diplomacy, empathy, and everything related to emotional intelligence. Most of this can be learned by simply paying attention to the people around you. Remember what Theodore Roosevelt said: "People don't care about what you know unless they know how much you care."

12.04 EMPLOYEE AND EMPLOYER'S MINDSET

The mass people can be divided into two categories.

- Employer and employee
- Leader and follower

All the great leaders who are leading the world are not necessarily a talented student in their schooling. Most of the talented students who get good marks in examination secure their higher position in competition and become very talented employees and work under an entrepreneur. Entrepreneurs are not a great performer in their schooling or at university examination, and many are back bencher and many are dropped out student in their school or college level. But they are leading the enterprises. The interesting thing is that they are using the talent of great performer of school and college. It means these talented people became employees of such people. The talent of a particular field is utilized by the dropped out students or those who were not so good at their schooling level.

The question is what is the basic difference in their pattern of thinking which makes a talented person just an employee under an entrepreneur. Both the persons have some different way of thinking. A talented man gets specialization in a particular field or in particular area, while entrepreneurs has specialization in hiring talented people and making investment to stand up a enterprise where the talents can be used to grow a concern into a big business empire. He uses the talents of different fields to grow up his business empire.

The vision of employee and employer are completely different. A student put his best efforts to get high grade and do some specialize education to get a good job. His prime focus is to prepare himself to get a best job. But the vision of an entrepreneur is something different. He doesn't dream to be an employee but think to start a business concern. Dream to be an employee or an employer is the basic difference in their thinking. This difference happens due to their basic concern.

- Employee type mindset has basic concern in job security. He bears a fear in his mind in taking any risk in life. He doesn't want to take any risk in his life. He never prefers risk and uncertainty in his career that is why he chooses to be an employee.
- Entrepreneur has basic concern about expansion of his business concern. He has a great desire to expand his business. He always thinks to start a new venture for increasing the cash flow in his life. The special quality is his ability to take risk. He has great expertise in hiring talented people for fulfilling his desire of expansion. These people play a pioneer role in building of society and country.
- Apart from risk-bearing capacity, they are a person of great vision. They visualize the great possibility well in advance and they adopt strategy in advance to utilize the opportunity for their expansion.
- They have great ability to hire talented person, to utilize their talents. They always expand their orbit.

- Their life style and vision revels that, talent doesn't make a man great but the ability to hire and use the talent makes a man great successful, and such people play a pioneer role always in the society.
- Many people start their career as an employee and learn the technique of the businessman for their profit and loss and later start their own venture by their experience as an employee and what they learned from their employer.
- Entrepreneur has great confidence on his ability to run a business concern. His confidence makes him capable to handle a big business concern and make it grow day by day.

My best advice to entrepreneurs is this: Forget about making mistake, just do it.

—Ajaero Tony Martins

In every success story, you will find someone who has made a courageous decision.

—Peter F. Drucker

12.05 REAL LEADERSHIP QUALITY

A very important line which defines completely, the real qualities of real leaders.

A real leader

- Knows the way
- Goes the way
- Shows the way

He identifies the leader

He makes them grow as prospective leaders.

It is not the great success of leaders, who have created huge followers. But the real leader is those who have really created great leader who are capable independently even in his absence.

A real leader identifies the potential of a follower and helps them to grow their potential at its optimum level.

12.06 HIGHLIGHTS OF THIS CHAPTER

1. To be rich or poor is just his mental belief and acceptance. His perception which is deeply rooted in his mind keeps him rich or poor.
2. Our love and appreciation to wealth attract wealth in our life. Negative feeling and approach towards wealth keep wealth away from our life.
3. Wealth plus high moral values bring peace and happiness in life. While wealth minus moral values makes our life unhappy and unpleasant.
4. What we give others returns back to our life in many folds. It is applicable to wealth also. Our effort to the creation of wealth and happiness to the life of employee's returns back to us in many fold bigger. This is applicable to both good and bad things in same way.
5. Specialized knowledge in any field give lots of wealth.
6. Risk-bearing capacity and foresight are main factors which differentiate the poor and rich people.
7. Poor people always thinks safe deposit scheme for the growth of their money, they live in fear mindset of losing money and that is why they never make any investment for financial growth.
8. Millionaire has a risk-bearing capacity and foresight that's why they make investment and their wealth grows

with high speed. And the most interesting thing is their money earns more money.

9. Poor people keeps on hard working life long in the expectation for accumulation of huge deposit, they lose their tendency to enjoy the wealth.

13. Miscellaneous

13.01 CATEGORY OF PEOPLE IN SOCIETY

CLASS I PEOPLE

- Very high moral values
- Very honest
- Justice for all feeling
- Law binding people
- Have concern for society and for country
- Big assets to society/country

CLASS II PEOPLE

- Low moral values
- Honesty level average
- Feeling of justice level low
- Respect for law, low
- Concern for society and country low
- Not too harmful for society/country

CLASS III PEOPLE

- Normal values
- Dishonest
- No feeling of justice
- No respect for law
- No concern towards society and country

- Big liability and problem for society/country
- 80% People have desire too much, but no work
- 15% People work for money, power and position
- 4% People work for skill and efficiency
- 1% People work for pleasure

13.02 STORY OF DASHRATH MANJHI

Dashrath Manjhi , also known as "Mountain Man", was a poor labourer in Gehlaur village, near Gaya in Bihar, India, who carved a path through a 360 ft long, 30 ft wide and 25 ft high hill block using only a hammer and chisel. After twenty-two years of work, Dashrath shortened the distance between the Atriand Wazirganj blocks of Gaya town from 55 km to 15 km.

Life of Dashrath Manjhi is a great example of great achievement, "where our will finds the way." It is a fact that he was just a labour who has to do work every day for his livelihood. But, the event of his wife's death during travel round the hill shocked and gave him a great strong reason for his life. The reason was so strong and clear and he was so passionate about this. Nothing could stop him. It is not easy to work for twenty-two years consistently, persistently with a great mission to create a path through the hill.

It is a great example of power of love. A true love has a great power of construction. When it goes in the wrong direction, this becomes a huge destructive thing. In real sense, his creation is really great since he had moved a mountain in his single handed efforts. His life proved a single man who is lacking for resources, but only due to his strong determination and great passion, how surpassed all the heart-breaking adverse and ultimately created path which will be convenient for the people of Gehlaur for generation to generation. The greatest thing is that his effort was not for his sole benefit, but he devoted his life for generation.

People in this world are busy for personal growth and personal goal. There are just a few who have great concern for their society and country. These people give the real sense of humanity. I think the real hero of mankind is Dashrath Manjhi and such people. His story is a great lesson to us. I found that the most important quality which makes him a great human being is his extremely strong determination power.

When we start any small or big venture, it doesn't start to give results. We have to keep on working and if your work develops up to a certain level then it starts to give some results. This phase when we keep on doing but the any result doesn't realize is a very crucial phase. When we get results, it is very easy to get motivated and perform with great enthusiasm. If we are not receiving any results after putting a great effort continuously, then it is a very difficult phase. Here strong resolution is the prime factor which makes a man sustain this dry period. As a whole, many ventures start and close within one year for not getting any considerable output within the period.

When Dashrath Manjhi started his mission alone, the starting years would have been very painful to him. His venture doesn't give considerable achievements. He completed his project after twenty-two years of heart-breaking labour without having sufficient resources and finance. He couldn't get support from local people and local administration. Although his mission was beneficial for the whole society, nobody gave him active and financial support. This reason is enough for anybody to stop the project, by thinking that nobody is supporting me in this great project, which is for the welfare of the society. But people's and administrations' indifferent approach towards his mission never made him dishearten. His consistent effort in cutting the hill just went on continuously. He never bothered whether the people and administration had taken interest or not in the project. He had only one picture in his mind, a road through the hill on which people are going to Atriand of Vajirganj Block. Earlier, people have to travel 55km, but now it remained only 15 km distance.

I salute Dashrath Manjhi for his so strong determination and resolution which made him capable to sustain in his mission having one man army type. When many people join a project, it is very easy to sustain. But, in this mission, he did everything all the time. Really, this is a great factor of this human being. His life teaches us some great qualities.

- You must have some great passion in your life
- You must have some great reason in your life
- Lack of resources doesn't matter much, if you have strong will power
- Your mission should have for the benefit of society and for mankind, not be limited for you and your family
- People may not give you much support, in starting phase but they all will associate with you on the completion of your project

Dashrath Manjhi is really a hero of our country, whose statue must be kept on the road cross. His unbelievable determination to work for the welfare of society, for so long period of twenty-two years is really unbelievable. It is very unfortunate if we don't pay respect and recognition to such a historical personality.

Albert Einstein said that a time will come when new generation we not believe that person of like Mahatma Gandhi was on the earth. Now I feel that really even now it is difficult to believe that a person having such strong determination and commitment worked consistently for twenty-two years and made a road through a mountain.

13.03 GENIUSES ARE MADE NOT BORN

Polgár's experiment with his daughters has been called "one of the most amazing experiments…in the history of human education." By his experiment he proved that geniuses are not born but they are made. He proved that any children if passes through a right training process from their early stage they can become a great performer in that particular field.

He wrote a book entitled *Bring up Genius!* He is also considered a pioneer theorist in child-rearing, who believes "geniuses are made, not born."

Geniuses are not born but they are made.

The experiment began in 1970 "with a simple premise: that any child has the innate capacity to become a genius in any chosen field, as long as education starts before their third birthday and they begin to specialize at six." Polgar "battled Hungarian authorities for permission" to home-school the girls." We didn't go to school, which was very unusual at the time," Judit recalled in 2008. "People would say, 'The parents are destroying them, they have to work all day, they have no childhood'. I became defensive, and not very sociable."

The family lived "in a modest apartment in the heart of Budapest" in which the "narrow living room" was "cluttered with chess books" and one wall was "lined with sketches of chess scenes from centuries ago." One account described it as "a shrine to unremitting chess practice. Thousands of chess books were stuffed onto shelves. Trophies and boards cluttered the living room. A file card system took up an entire wall. It included records of previous games for endless analytical pleasure and even an index of potential competitors' tournament histories."

Polgár began teaching his eldest daughter, Susan, to play chess when she was four years old. "Six months later, Susan toddled into Budapest's smoke-filled chess club", which was crowded with elderly men, and proceeded to beat the veteran players. "Soon thereafter, she dominated the city's girls-under-age-eleven tournament with a perfect score." Judit was able to defeat her father at chess when she was just five." For me, learning chess was natural; with my sisters around me, I wanted to play," said Judit in 2008. The family, she noted, had been the target of "some vicious anti-Semitism" during the girls' childhood. At age twelve, she "got a letter, with a picture of my father with his eyes [gouged] out; and very nasty words." Largely because of the anti-Semitism and criticism they had to endure, there was "no jealousy" among the sisters; Judit said in 2008 that these challenges "kept us bound together."

In 2012, Judit told an interviewer about the "very special atmosphere" in which she had grown up. "In the beginning it was a game. My father and mother are exceptional pedagogues who can motivate and tell it from all different angles. Later, chess for me became a sport, an art, a science, everything together. I was very focused on chess, and happy with that world. I was not the rebelling and going out type. I was happy that at home we were a closed circle and then we went out playing chess and saw the world. It's a very difficult life and you have to be very careful, especially the parents, who need to know the limits of what you can and can't do with your child. My parents spent most of their time with us; they travelled with us [when we played abroad], and were in control of what was going on. With other prodigies it might be different. It is very fragile. But I'm happy that with me and my sisters it didn't turn out in a bad way." A reporter for *the Guardian* noted that unlike many top chess players, who are dysfunctional, the adult Judit was "relaxed, approachable and alarmingly well balanced," having managed "to juggle a career in competitive chess with having two young children, running a chess foundation in Hungary, writing books and developing educational programmes based on chess."

13.04 DR A P J ABDUL KALAM LIFE

Kalam had average grades but was described as a bright and hardworking student who had a strong desire to learn, in his school years. He spent hours on his studies, especially mathematics. While Kalam was working on a senior class project, the Dean was dissatisfied with his lack of progress and threatened to revoke his scholarship unless the project was finished within the next three days. Kalam met the deadline, impressing the Dean, who later said to him, "I was putting you under stress and asking you to meet a difficult deadline." He narrowly missed achieving his dream of becoming a fighter pilot, as he placed ninth in qualifiers, and only eight positions were available.

His life rally gives great message to us and a great human being on which all we Indian feel proud for him. As the fact he was not an extraordinary student in brilliancy, however his dedication and involvement to mathematics was really extra ordinary.

A very big misconception is gradually developing in the mind of new generation that without manipulation and contact nobody can achieve some higher big achievement in life. Second thing they think high moral value becomes obstacle in great achievement. These two negative perceptions attract our younger generation to make them involve in unfair activities and gradually corruption are growing in the mindset of new generations. Dr Kalam's life clearly shows that he was from a very poor family. He had to sell newspaper for some extra income to support his parents' livelihood. He is really a great role model for not only India but for worldwide. The unique qualities which made him so beloved President of India are

- Dedication to his subject mathematics and physics.
- Great moral values in life
- Great dreamer
- Simplicity and humanity feeling

LIFE IS A GAME OF CARD

So how does one become skilled in the playing of cards? I believe it starts with a good attitude. Then you need to pay attention. Each card game is different, and the players change. We haven't even gotten to regional variations or even 'house rules,' where things are a little different because of where you are playing.

You can get better by practicing. You can get better by observing what good players do or don't do, and in what circumstances. You can get better by reading books of good players. You can get better by understanding the odds and probabilities of the game. You can get better by practicing some more.

While all of these apply directly to card games, they apply to life as well. Whatever you are trying to do, someone has done something similar before. Find that person, or a book about that person, and learn from their triumphs and from their mistakes. As kids, we learn from others (hopefully good examples of what to do), and imitate them.

How do you get better at something? Some people like to learn by doing, others prefer a mentor, or at least a good book. Sometimes, it depends on your comfort level, and the risk involved in trying something. Before I was ready to skydive, it took a former military dive master to talk me into it.

We all have our hands to play. What is in yours at the moment? What are your high cards, and your low cards? What do you have for structure (runs, straights, flushes, pairs, etc.)? Most importantly, what is your next play? Do you know what you're going to do with that hand?

Some people spend more time planning than playing, and others just play whatever comes to mind with little thought. As usual, I believe the best path is somewhere between these extremes. There is a place for planning, and there is a place for intuition or inspiration.

What can you do to maximize your 'hand' at home, at work, with your friends, with your family and in other social organizations? For me, the more interesting question is what can you do to help others with your hand? I don't mean letting someone else win, but can you mentor them? Help them understand, or play their cards better?

Cards are not the best analogy for life, in my opinion. The wages is fixed, and for someone to win, the others must lose. I don't believe life is a zero sum game, or the wealthiest people in the history of the world would have been the first ones to call themselves human, because we've been subdividing the spoils ever since.

I believe it is both possible, ethical, and practical to help others learn how to play the game better. We are rarely in direct competition with anyone (or put differently, there are far more people we do not compete with than those with which we do compete).

Play, practice, and learn. Get better, and help others get better. We can all win the game of life, if we play our hands right. We have at least that much free will. Well, at least I think I do, how about you?

13.05 LIFE OF JAYA DEVI (RAIN WATER HARVESTING)

How Jaya Devi was just twelve when she got married. Like many others, she could have just remained another child bride of Bihar. But she chose a different path.

From fighting with Naxalites to planting trees and doing rain water harvesting, Jaya Devi is truly the "Green Lady" of Bihar. She not only went on to change her life but also led to the development of her entire village one day, during a regular medical check-up, she shared her desire to bring a change with the nurse. The lady advised her to form a group as fighting alone in Bihar was not an easy task. She then set up a self-help group in 1997 in Saradhi village of Bihar to help marginalized communities, especially women, avoid money lenders and become financially independent.

She started with bringing women together and helping them save money. She enabled women to educate themselves, send their children to school and take advantage of already existing schemes of the government. The main problem with the village was that there was no source of income. They were dependent on rain which was very uneven. That is when they started rain water harvesting.

She met a social worker from a nearby village, who introduced her to the various methods of rain water conservation. Jaya brought the villagers together and constructed a tank to catch the rain water. She also managed to get people to give "sramdaan" (voluntary labour who contribute his work for social cause) and construct the tank all by themselves. Her efforts started to gradually show results.

To take their efforts to a new level, the villagers laid an 800-ft pipeline to bring water from the Kareli hills to the ground. This project was a huge success and gave a good boost to agricultural growth in that low rainfall area.

Her love for nature enabled her to spread awareness about tree plantation, and she, along with the help of the villagers, planted over one lakh trees in her village and nearby areas.

In the future she wanted to educate all the children, stop child marriage and provide safety to the villagers. They have been living in threat their entire lives due to the Naxalites. With the support of the people and the government she hoped to fight this.

Her life picture is very clear that "you find the way." It doesn't depend on how much resources you have in your life, but the things which matters is how strong is the desire in your mind. How you feel pain for the people who are under privileged. Those who work in society especially for the development of the life of poor and exploited people have some special qualities which make them different from other people.

They have a deep in satisfaction for the prevailed situation.

They have a risk-bearing capacity to fight against the whole system.

They don't compromise with the present system.

They are not concentrated to the welfare for his family only but they think for the welfare of whole society.

The level of humanity in their mind is very high, which makes them capable to think humanity as whole.

Upliftment of the life of under privileged people really gives happiness to such people.

13.06 TOO MUCH ANALYSIS BRINGS PARALYSIS

Our success and pleasure both are very deeply related to others. We start many programs in our life and many of them are completed while many of them fail at any stage and we have to postpone due to many reasons. But at the time of starting we think about the successful completion. For successful completion of any program we take care of our best for making it 100% successful. We analyse all the pros and cons and the probable problem may come in the path of the project. For this reason, we analyse all the aspects of probable problems and their solution. This is a precautionary major which is taken to make the project successful.

Many times we devote much time and energy in analysing the work process instead of taking action for further progress. Many cases the process of analysis becomes too much which hampers our movement and our action part. We cannot predict the entire probable problem and their solution on the beginning of the project. Many problems and their solution will come when required in the process of action. But our fearful mind and too much analytical approach make it difficult to take action. Later on it becomes tendency to analyse more and more which decrease our ability to act. In the process of analysis a lot of options are being considered, and our mind gets trapped in a cycle to find out more and more better solution.

As our analytical behaviour increases, our ability to action decreases day by day. A time comes that analysis becomes our compulsion and changes it into a mania of thinking too much. Any activity when it becomes a mania, then it is a stage of disease.

This disease affects our ability to act worst. We start making big plans and modify the plan of action in a very decent way but all are futile since it chokes our ability to action. His uncontrolled thinking just keeps on going about the action plan and many new and attractive plans develop but all are useless since the ability to act gets paralysed.

Initially this habit develops very slowly, and it appears that it is very good to find a perfect plan, but for many people it becomes a mania just to analyse the plan of action. Similar to all the disease it is realized only when it is deeply established in mind. Then it is very difficult to come out from this compulsive behaviour.

13.07 A FLUTE MANUFACTURER

A boy saw a very beautiful flute and he was so impressed with it, he made his mission to manufacture such a beautiful flute, which has not been prepared so far. He went out from his home and started a rigorous search for perfect bamboo pieces to manufacture master pieces. In this process he travelled jungle to jungle and many states in the search of a perfect piece of bamboo. In this process he spent many year of his life, ultimately he found the coveted piece of bamboo after a long search. He was extremely happy and started to manufacture his masterpiece flute. It took several years, since he wants to make it unique things, so that anybody who will hear will be surprised on the beauty of the flute. At last he finished his great task actually which was his mission. His focus and involvement and the beauty of the flute became a matter of attraction and people started to come to see the marvellous preparation which took his many valuable years. It was greatly appreciated by the visitors and his happiness was at the climax since his dream ultimately came true.

One day a saint came to him and saw his flute and said it is beautiful. Then he asked him to play the flute, but he couldn't play it properly. The saint was frustrated on his performance and asked him that you have devoted your life on the manufacturing of a beautiful flute which is a secondary thing and you have missed the prime thing is to play the flute. You were focused on secondary thing so much that you have completely missed the primary purpose of the flute. Actually you have wasted your life in secondary thing only.

This story shows how we waste our valuable years in non-essential things and we mis completely the primary goal of life. He missed the basic purpose of the flute to create a melody song. Day by day he fascinated with the beauty of the flute and day by day he kept on adding new decoration and perfection in the flute but never practiced a song by flute.

Now many conclusions can be derived from this beautiful story.

- We need to understand what is the primary and what is the secondary
- Many times, it happens that we waste our life for secondary things and miss the primary objective
- Our repeated action becomes our habit, and later on it converted to compulsion
- Focus on particular area expands in our life

This is just a story showing how we focus a devotee of valuable time energy and focus on non-essential things and we missed the actual purpose of life. Happiness and satisfaction are the main propose of life and money is just the media by which we get happiness and satisfaction. But most of the cases most of the person starts to earn money for happiness and satisfaction but gradually they miss the actual purpose of life. And earning money becomes the prime focus of life. They compromise from their happiness and satisfaction and the use all the legal and illegal means to earn money. In this process, they don't realize how their so much affinity creates unhappy and unsatisfied situation which is almost impossible to reverse back.

A person stars to earn money for him and his family requirements. The basic thought is that after earning, his family life will be comfortable and they will not suffer for the need of money. So, he starts to do hard work for earning money. By the time he involves in the process, he doesn't care for his rest and not care for his health. Actually in this stage he starts enjoying the game of earning money. The rate of earning of money is slow but gradually the rate of earning grows and it brings enjoying things. It is a fact that achievements have its own passion and motivation. This involvement makes him so much involved and focused that nothing gives him pleasure except money earning.

He does not realize that his prime focus shifted to money earning since he started to enjoy earning money. Gradually he creates ample of money and another problem attracted his life related to money. Now another problem starts how to protect and increase the money. This is a never ending trap in which he trapped completely and until death he can't come out from this trap.

In the mean time in the process of money earning he has lost his health and earned huge money. Now on growing the careless life style gave many health problems. Huge money is being spent on the recovery of treatment.

It can be summarized as "He has lost his health for earning money and later age he is losing money to gain health." At last the net result is zero.

- In this incident we see that the boy gradually devoted himself in modification and beautification of the flute. It gradually became his habit and later on it became compulsion. Although it is difficult to come out from the compulsion, but there is way to come out. Three factors are important components which form our habit.

- Our focus
- Our energy
- Our time

On deep analysis, we came to the point that we pay these three components in more or less quantity which form our habit and tendency. They are just like water, ground, and manure which are the three components important things for the growth of any plants. These three things combine for a balanced growth of a plant. Deficiency in any one thing will affect the plant adversely since all the three processes are required to complete growth.

13.08 HOW COOPERATION MAKES ANYTHING EASY?

Fifty people gathered in a hall, and fifty balloons have been given to them. They advised that they have to write their names on the balloon. All the balloons were kept beside the room. They had been suggested that they have to find out their balloon which are jumbled and kept besides the room within three minutes. There was one condition that nobody has to help other, they have to search their own balloon only and come back. After three minutes, all backed with empty hands. Surprisingly nobody could be able to find their balloon.

Now a little change has been made in this game. Now they are allowed to help each other. All they rushed to the room and started to find out the balloon, and they started to call the person whose name was written in the balloon and this way all the fifty people were able to find out their own balloon due to the mindset of helping other.

This is a very interesting example how our happiness and success is associated with others. This story shows very clearly that our helping attitude to others returns back to us in many ways.

- ✦ So the moral is to come out from the mindset to work for our own happiness and success. Feel and understand how our happiness is associated with the happiness of other people.

13.09 DESIRE OF GREAT PEOPLE

- ✦ An average person dreams for money
- ✦ An ambitious dreams for power and positions
- ✦ Contribute great dreams to the society and country

I don't want to project myself smart and rich by wearing borrowed coat and tie from others. I have no coat and no costly dresses; despite I am very happy and satisfied with my dresses.

- ✦ The person who has courage to do things has no power
- ✦ Those who have power to do have no courage
- ✦ Those who have both power and courage democracy makes them helpless to do soothing great for the country

Difficulties can be used as an excuse,

Or can be used for sharpening your skill.

The question is you are making excuses or sharpening your skills.

The stone that bears the pain of a chisel and hammer becomes a statue which is worshiped. A marble which couldn't hear the pain of chisel and hammer is used for the marble stone of steps of staircase.

In electricity transmission some quantity of electricity is wasted during the transmission. System is modified to minimize the wastage of electricity during transmission. Similarly all of our efforts are not converted to result, so learn to increase our productivity by minimizing our wastage.

Our hydroelectric projects are an excellent example which shows how the waters are stored whole year and how it provides water and produces electricity whole year by moving turbines.

- Happy and unhappy are not two different things, the difference of intensity increases becomes happy and decreases become unhappy
- Hot and cold are not two things, they are just the high and low intensity of heat. High intensity of heat becomes hot and low intensity becomes cold
- Honesty and dishonesty
- Rich and poor
- Light and dark
- There is just a difference in intensity but there is nothing anything like dark. There is only one thing that is light and its low intensity or absence is called dark

In any organization you will have to work with both good and bad people. Working with good people gives pleasure and work becomes enjoyable whereas work with bad people gives experience. They sharpen our skill to handle such difficult people and difficult situation. No situation is bad, you can learn and earn from any situation either good or bad.

13.10VALUE ADDITION IN OUR ACTIVITIES

Everybody knows that morning walking is very essential for good health, but just a few people among which many are a diabetic patient used to walk on a regular basis. As per doctor's suggestion at least one should have a brisk walk and 30–40 minutes is sufficient for a diabetic patient. When we walk only by keeping the fact to complete 30–40 minutes, then this work will be very monotonous and boring and will be difficult to continue. However, if we do it daily only to complete 30–40 minutes, then it is just like a punishment. Simply we can add some value in this morning walk and can make it very joyful act. My simple purpose is to make any activity which we have to do for any reason we must make it a joyful act by value addition in the activity. Many things we can add as value addition.

1. It is an opportunity to get up in early morning
2. It is an opportunity to take high oxygen for better health
3. Discipline is increasing in my life
4. Pain-bearing capacity is increasing
5. At morning nature looks most beautiful

13.11 DEVELOP A COMFORTABLE APPROACH IN EVERY SITUATION

Human civilization has been developed from Stone Age to the age of rocket age. Between these developments we have crossed many big milestones in human civilization. Vehicle has been advanced from ox-cart vehicle to high speed cars, bullet trains and rocket. Our invention has made our vehicle too much efficient, powerful and fuel efficient, after all speed has increased very much.

Technology has made everything in our life very fast. Before information age, we used write letters for communication. We have to wait at least 10 days to get any reply from other side. There was no any option. Communication became very advance and it became cheaper and efficient greatly. These are just an example how we get any information within few minutes and we can reach anywhere within few hours.

All of these developments have created a panic situation in our mind to do anything very fast. The whole generation is almost suffering this panic mental situation. Everyone is putting his best efforts to live behind all. Involvement of so large people in such a mental and physical behaviour created a big rest in which all are running so that he couldn't be left behind and the most ambitious people thinks to keep himself most ahead in this race. Overall all are living in a panic situation. To be in a panic mood has become very common these days.

Talented and ambitious people are in tension to keep them first in this race while average people are in tension, not to be left behind in the huge race. This race has stolen peace of our life. It has stolen our comfort of our life. This panic mind state has polluted every sphere of our life. Everyone is running such a way he has to reach there in first position. If he reaches there 5–10 minutes later some big miss happening will occur. Basically all of these happen due to our extreme focus on our goal. Of course goal is important but the process must also be joyful which makes our achievement perfect.

Now the need of time is to develop our approach to be comfortable in every situation. Many have developed a panic approach due to the environment where we live, the association with whom we deal; all of these have stolen our comfortable approach in life. We have to reinstate our comfortable way of dealing, which is a prime requirement of a happy and joyful life.

Our unrest behaviour is deeply associated with our breathing pattern. Everyone knows our breathing is affected by our mental state. When we are in fearful or excited state, then the speed of our breathing increases abruptly. When we are in a comfortable and peaceful mood, our breathing speed becomes very normal and rhythmic. Most of us do not know that we can change our mind by our mood by making our breathing in rhythm. In yoga and pranayam there are a number of techniques which are practiced to keep our breathing pattern in rhythm. There are a lot of things which change our life in a very positive way by practicing very simple techniques on a regular basis. Many times we don't pay attention which can be done in an easy way, without paying much money, but our mindset doesn't believe on that a complicated process. There is also a fact that we are ready to pay thousands of rupees for medical treatment through doctors but it is difficult to do a few simple exercises which has great impact on our health but in a gradual manner. It doesn't create miracle in just a few days. It takes time and requires regular practice. These things develop in our life in a gradual manner and last long and are very effective. However, the main problem which lies in our mind is we want results immediately. He has no patience to do a particular exercise on a regular basis. Our impatient approach is the root cause of different problems in our life.

So, this is the need of the time to develop comfortable approach of dealing everything in our life. It is just a skill to keep ourselves cool and comfortable. Suppose I have to travel 500 km to reach my destination. This distance can be travelled in panic way, in which I will drive my vehicle at high speed and will avoid halting on the way to take rest and for cooling process of the vehicle. Overheating of engine will decrease the efficiency and power of the vehicle. I will save a few hours but it will create tension and a painful journey. Life risk is also involved in this journey. In other way I can travel this journey in a very comfortable manner. Of course, I will have to spend a few hours more but it will be joyful, fuel efficient and risk will be less.

We can increase our efficiency by adopting a comfortable manner of working. This is just a habit which can be developed by regular practice.

What we think at the time of our action is mostly responsible which make us comfortable or uncomfortable.

13.12 JESIKA COKS

She was born without hands but she never treated herself helpless. She is the first pilot in world history aviation who is flying a plane by her feet. She got black belt title in Tie Kwando. She is now thirty-two years old.

Her name got registered in Greenish Book of record in 2008 when she got licence for flying plane. These are the facts about the first pilot who got licence to fly a plane who is physically handicapped. Now, a most important fact comes out from her life and determination power.

First I think the level of her determination and will power which never bow down even without hands from her birth. She never accepted defeat even after having a big physical disability. Her life is a great example of overcoming the inability. She had chosen a most challenging job of flying a plane to prove that nothing can stop one if she has strong determination and will power. She had conveyed this message to this world by her name entered in Greenish Book of world record.

This is a great example how an individual do not accept defeat despite a big physical disability. This shows her fighting spirit against the challenges. Her fighting spirit is unparalleled. Our fighting spirit against the challenges is the most deciding factor which makes a man winner or loser. So it is not the resource but the inner fighting strength which decides our destiny and fate.

This is a unique example of strong determination and commitment. In our society and work place always we meet people who are physically fit but at mental level they are handicapped. They have no inner strength to fight against the situation, and there life is a crippling.

"Either you take your challenges to make yourself motivated or you may use it for an excuse"

Sudha Chandran a famous film star lost her leg in an accident. It was normally impossible to be a big dancer with her artificial Jaipur foot. But her strong determination and strong fighting spirit against the challenges made her a winner. Her passion for a classical dance came true only due to her passion and determination for a dance.

13.13 HIGHLIGHTS OF THIS CHAPTER

1. Different category people always live in the society who works for and against the society according to their quality and nature.
2. Even less than 1% of people work for pleasure.
3. Even now it is difficult to believe that there was a person Dashrath Manjhi who had worked like a one man army and built a road through a hill by consistent work for twenty-two years.
4. Polgar proved by his experiment that genius are not born but made. He proved that any children can be a genius in any field if he is trained at very early stage.
5. Dr A P J Abdul Kalam was very average in his early school but his dedication and discipline for his study was unparalleled by which he became a "Missile man for India" and later on he became the President of India.
6. A boy devoted his whole life for developing beauty in his flute but he never paid interest in playing flute which was the primary goal of the purpose. Peace of mind is primary and money is secondary, but for most of the person money becomes primary and peace of mind becomes secondary.
7. Our helping attitude to others returns back to us in many forms.
8. Our desire shows our level of thinking and personality. It is a well-established fact that average and below average people always concerned for their welfare while great people always concerned for the mass people specially for the under privileged people.

9. We feel comfortable in living in our comfort zone. But if we don't expand our comfort zone then it decreases. Living in our comfort zone, our skill and ability decreases day by day. So, expand your comfort zone daily.